SPEAKING OF TRAINS

This is an IndieMosh book

brought to you by MoshPit Publishing
an imprint of Mosher's Business Support Pty Ltd

PO Box 4363
Penrith NSW 2750

indiemosh.com.au

Copyright © Jim Nicholls 2022

The moral right of the author has been asserted in accordance with the Copyright Amendment (Moral Rights) Act 2000.

All rights reserved. Except as permitted under the Australian Copyright Act 1968 (for example, fair dealing for the purposes of study, research, criticism or review) no part of this publication may be reproduced, stored in a retrieval system, or transmitted in any form or by any means, electronic, mechanical, photocopying, recording or otherwise, without the written permission of the publisher.

 A catalogue record for this work is available from the National Library of Australia

https://www.nla.gov.au/collections

Title:	Speaking of Trains
Author:	Nicholls, Jim
ISBNs:	9781922912121 (paperback) 9781922912138 (ebook – epub) 9781922912145 (ebook – Kindle)
Subjects:	NON-FICTION: Travel / General; HISTORY / Africa West.

This book is a memoir. It reflects the author's present recollections of experiences over time. All persons within are actual individuals; there are no composite characters. The names of some individuals have been changed to respect their privacy.

Cover concept by Jim Nicholls.

Cover design and layout by Ally Mosher at allymosher.com.

Cover images used from Jim Nicholls.

All photographs are copyright Jim Nicholls with the exception of the postcard of the Herero massacre in Chapter 1 (Courtesy of South African History Online).

SPEAKING OF TRAINS

JIM NICHOLLS

The Runaway Rattler by Jim Nicholls.

Book Review by Colin Taylor, author of *Traincatcher*.

Many have contemplated travelling right round the world since the successful Magellan expedition of 1519-1522. Jules Verne's Phileas Fogg sought to do it in 80 days, and actually took only 79 because of the International Date Line. His trip was made possible only by, among other things, the opening of the American Transcontinental Railway in 1869 and the Suez Canal that same year.

The National Geographic Magazine in 1951 (Vol C, No 6) describes a round-world trip in 80 days by Newman Bumstead, but only six were spent in travelling, mostly by air. The rest of his time was seeing places and meeting people. Lone sailors have done it by yacht, it has been attempted by balloon, 'Photogypsy' Almitra Von Wilcox is doing it on foot, and still walking, but Jim Nicholls of Laidley, Queensland, dreamt of doing it by train.

The problem, for Jim as well as Almitra, is that there were a few gaps which neither Shanks' Pony nor trains can cross. True, the English Channel had been tunnelled, but crossings of some wider stretches of water had yet to be constructed or even contemplated – so there had to be some parts of the trip where not even a 'Runaway Rattler' was there for the would-be circumnavigator.

In fact, right at the start Jim had a problem. There was no train from Laidley: Queensland Rail had taken away the daily railcar to Brisbane some years back. In actual fact there was a train that stopped at Laidley – but only to pick up for the dead-end line to southwest Queensland, which would mean backtracking to the starting point – hardly the right way to begin an epic journey.

And epic journey it was. In a period of around 80 days – he was not racing to do it in a given time – Jim travelled over 47,000 kilometres by 40-odd trains which varied from real old rattlers to modern high-speed expresses like the *Eurostar* and comfortable cruise trains like the *California Zephyr* and Australia's own *Indian Pacific*.

Like Homer's Ulysses before him, "many cities did he visit and many were the nations with whose manners and customs he was acquainted." And they were all interesting, especially the people, from conductress "Grumble Bum" in Vietnam to the elusive but tantalising Erica whom he met in Thailand.

This is a book not just for train buffs. Although basic facts are given, the book is not cluttered with technical details like the number of driving wheels of locomotives. It is more of an adventure story, like Tschiffely's Ride on horseback through South America, in parts reminiscent of Eric Newby's *The Big Red Train Ride* but more varied and interesting – a worthy successor to Paul Theroux's *The Great Railway Bazaar* and covering more countries.

Jim's lone adventure encompassed New Zealand, the USA, Canada, Britain, France, Belgium, Germany, Poland, Belarus, Russia, China, Vietnam, Thailand, Malaysia, Singapore and finally Australia from Perth to Brisbane. Jim enjoyed meeting people and, while critical of some of the trains and railway managements (who isn't?), he has good words to say of his human encounters. His obvious enjoyment of the whole trip communicates itself to the reader.

Although the trip necessarily included some air hops and the occasional bus or taxi, Jim's odyssey included one of the longest possible rail journeys in the world: from Kyle of Lochalsh in the Scottish Highlands to Hanoi in Vietnam, over 16,000 kilometres.

Of all the trains, Jim reckoned Amtrak's *Coast Starlight* in the USA about the best, and the *XPT* of New South Wales was clearly among the worst, although he qualifies this by concluding that "there is no such thing as a bad train", or as poet and rail traveller Edna St Vincent Millay so aptly put it:

"My heart is warm with the friends I make,
And better friends I'll not be knowing,
Yet there isn't a train I wouldn't take,
No matter where it's going."

Jim has previously written of train journeys in both *The Queensland Times* and the former *Valley Times* newspapers.

His book is a great read.

Contents

Introduction 1

Chapter One: The Pride of Africa 3

Chapter Two: The Hudson Bay 43

Chapter Three: Riding a Typhoon in Vietnam 56

Chapter Four: Riding the Lhasa Limited 68

Chapter Five: Three Chinese Cities 80

Chapter Six: The Royal Way to Rajasthan 96

Chapter Seven: New Zealand.. 118

Also by Jim Nicholls 132

About the author.. 133

Introduction

My fascination with trains began during my childhood in the grand old railway town of Cootamundra in southern New South Wales. It was there that I grew up beside the main line linking Sydney and Melbourne, spending what now seem to have been endless days in a whirl of fantasy and awe watching the mighty steam engines and their glamourous trains taking people away to exotic places. Those exotic places may only have been Sydney or Melbourne, but to a ten-year-old boy looking up at trains from a lonely level crossing, there was an air of romance and mystery about them that I was unable to find in my bucolic birthplace.

Even now when ensconced in one of those delightful mobile cubby houses, I am overwhelmed by a feeling of privacy and extreme cosiness that is almost childlike. God is in heaven, nations are at peace, all's well with the world.

No other form of transport has ever come near to creating such an aura of romance and excitement as that presented by the railways. Although cars and aircraft may be convenient and have now removed much of the thrill and gloss and nostalgia from long distance travel, noxious motor cars, stuffy buses and claustrophobic aeroplanes will never offer the same feeling of luxury and smugness, and the spirit of adventure that a train journey brings.

Train travel also opens a window on the world, allowing a visual eavesdropping and intrusion into a country's backyard that, if it was done in any other form, would probably result in arrest. With no feelings of guilt one can become a blatant voyeur at large and can peer unashamedly over the back fences of the world, and into the lives of strangers. Life, no matter how indiscreet and indelicate, is played out for all to see on the far side of a carriage window.

Perhaps the most pleasurable experience of all that is pleasurable about being on board a train is meeting new and interesting people. Strangers on a train tend to tell each other things they would never dream of saying if they were anywhere else. I'm sure it has something to do with the realisation that once their secrets have been offloaded, they know (or indeed hope) they will never see you again.

Modern train travellers tend to have something in common: an appreciation of all things to do with railways and a sense of belonging to a community that, for the duration of the journey at least, is isolated and insulated from the outside world.

Trains have it all, they convert the journey into the adventure. Real people travel on trains.

Weeks away from home and thousands of kilometres along the Trans-Siberian Railway, this same subject was the core of discussion among a group of strangers in a cramped compartment on a Russian train. A young girl from New Zealand, taking the long way home, whom I had never met until then, neatly summed it up: ... 'Yeah, how many nice people do you ever meet on an aeroplane?'

Chapter One: The Pride of Africa

Introduction

This magnificent train travels from Swakopmund in Namibia, the former German colony of South West Africa to Pretoria, the administrative capital of the Republic of South Africa.

The train regards itself as the world's most luxurious, and I have no doubt it could well be; luxury and I have never had much of a relationship. However, I'm prepared to persevere with it as the only means of enjoying a long ride on a South African train and coming to grips with a journey through unfamiliar territory.

Just getting myself to the train's departure point, Swakopmund in Namibia, became an adventure within itself: no direct flights and no local trains. And, of course, the railway people have nothing to offer in the way of help or suggestions. You just somehow get yourself there. Which then has me wondering about those passengers who are taking the one-way trip from Pretoria – travelling from east to west. How do they get back to the big city after they have been dislodged from the train at its western terminus? At least I won't be facing that particular dilemma.

Before becoming an independent nation in 1990, Namibia was known as German South West Africa, a colony of the German Empire from 1884 until 1915. With an area of more than eight hundred and thirty-five thousand square kilometres, it was one and a half times the size of the mainland German Empire in Europe at the time. In 1915, during the First World War, German South West Africa was invaded by the Western Allies in the form of South African and British forces. After the war its administration was taken over by the Union of South Africa, part of the British Empire, and the territory was administered as South West Africa under a League of Nations mandate.

Swakopmund

Despite having to overcome earlier dramas and mishaps mainly to do with missing luggage (courtesy of South African Airways) and a camera that was lost twice but found only once, I have finally reached the Atlantic Ocean town of Swakopmund in western Namibia. Swakopmund is a city of around thirty thousand citizens, and a place I had never before heard of, unaware that it even existed until I began planning this trip. It wins me over at first sight. And don't try pronouncing the name with a mouthful of Jatz crackers. With several days to spare before the train is due to depart from here, I have an excellent chance to look around this place where its German influence and heritage is on show at every opportunity. From street signs, to the names written above the shopfronts, to the language people speak, everything reflects the days of German colonisation, even though that all disappeared one hundred years ago.

    Arrival at Swakopmund by bus from Windhoek in growing darkness. I check into the Dunedin Star Guest House. No beer or mini bar in the room. But the young girl at reception is sympathetic to my plight and is quite agreeable to escorting me to a backpacker hostel around the corner and down an unlit street where she introduces me to Freddie the barman. This is an interesting place; the bar is situated on an upper level, accessed by a spiral staircase. Easy enough to get up to, but a bit of a challenge on the return journey.

It grows much darker and the night is becoming colder. A thin fog rolls in from the Atlantic Ocean.

In the morning light, the beauty of this town and its German heritage is on full view. The streets and footpaths are so clean and neat that I could be forgiven for thinking this is not a part of Africa. It is a delight: wide streets and clean and tidy gardens. No graffiti, no dogs on the loose, no noise. Although the German South West Africans were cut off politically from Germany in 1915 at the beginning of the First World War, and despite being alone and isolated for a century, they have successfully maintained their language, culture and society through any number of tough times. Since the introduction of home satellite service, television has been their only cultural, lingual and informational link with the Fatherland, but they don't look or sound any different from ... dare I say, German-Germans?

Namibia is the only African country that has a daily German language newspaper. People speak in a mixture of English and German: 'Thank you' becomes 'Dankie', and a 'Good morning' on my part invariably brings forth a cheery 'Guten Morgen'. The townsfolk are friendly and polite and, as the young waiter says to me in a coffee shop one morning: 'There is no war or fighting going on here, everyone is friends.'

A bit different to the rest of the continent, I think to myself.

This is all very well, but as the days roll on and I get to talk to more people and learn more about this part of the world, a very different picture begins to emerge. Although I will get to that later on, at the moment I am just happy to be looking around and exploring such a charming town.

Swakopmund shopfront

Swakopmund was founded in 1892, two years later than Windhoek, the Namibian capital. On 4 August of that year the crew of the German gunboat *Hyena* erected two beacons to mark the landing site which symbolised the laying of the town's foundation stone. The first building, a barracks for the troops was erected the following month. German South West Africa was the descriptive, and not very imaginative, name given to their new colony.

The Berlin Conference of 1883 advocated that Africa should be divided up between various European nations, anyone wanting a slice of the action, just rock up and take whatever you want. Understandably, this all came as a bit of a surprise to the Africans. Slow off the mark, Germany ended up with this arid desert land that most Europeans avoided, seeing little point in bothering with it. By dubious means, either purchase or theft or both, the Germans gradually gained control of the central and southern parts of the territory. One of the methods the Germans used to gain control was to offer 'protection' in exchange for land. But this failed miserably when one of the strong local leaders Hendrik Witbooi hit back and stole the horses of the Imperial Commissioner Doctor Heinrich Goering, father of the future Nazi Air Marshall Hermann Goering. The way things were going, it seemed as though the Germans, rather than the locals, were the ones in need of protection.

As the main deep water harbour at Walvis Bay, located thirty-three kilometres to the south, was already in British hands, increased traffic between Germany and its South West African colony necessitated establishing a port of its own. With other sites deemed to be unsuitable, or already snapped up, the choice fell on Swakopmund. As there was no natural harbour, ships had to anchor about one kilometre out from the shoreline. Livestock, horses or heavy cargo was off-loaded onto rafts or special surf boats designed to negotiate the heavy seas. Kroo tribesmen had been using similar methods on the Liberian coast for many years, and teams of these skilled boatmen were brought to Swakopmund under contract to 'work the surf'. At the height of these operations the Woermann Line employed nearly six hundred Kroo men. This method of off-loading from the rafts and boats was so effective, it was continued well after a jetty had been constructed.

In 1898 a government-appointment architect arrived to oversee the construction of an artificial harbour basin. Accompanied by great celebrations the Swakopmund Mole Harbour was officially opened by Governor Friedrich von Lindequist on 12 February 1903. A set of rail tracks carrying three steam cranes ran the length of the Mole. Tugs would tow rafts into the safety of the harbour basin where, protected from the high surf, the cranes could hoist the loads to safety. The number of vessels offloading at Swakopmund increased rapidly. In 1894 four ships offloaded; in 1896, a bimonthly service was introduced by the Woermann Line. This became a monthly service in 1899.

The Herero uprising of January 1904 exacerbated the problem as the need for essential extra military supplies increased. At times, up to twenty vessels could be lying at anchor in the Swakopmund roadway awaiting offloading. Between 1904 and 1906, eleven thousand horses were landed in this manner, and by the outbreak of the Great War, thirty-one thousand horses and thirty-four thousand mules had been moved through the port of Swakopmund.

The available dredging equipment proved to be inadequate and port authorities were working twenty-four hours a day in their attempts to alleviate the situation. It was decided to build a landing jetty on the southern side of the Mole. Within a year, landing operations at the Mole were suspended in favour of the newly-built wooden jetty. Today the Mole is one of the town's focal points and one of its main attractions, containing as it does a sheltered beach, parks, palm-lined walkways, hotels, shops, restaurants, a swimming pool and museum.

The names given to places by the original inhabitants were very descriptive and in many instances those names were retained by European settlers who sometimes simplified the pronunciation. The name Swakopmund is derived from the Nama word Tsoakhaub meaning 'excrement opening' describing the Swakop River in flood as it carried putrid water full of mud, sand, pieces of rotting vegetation and dead animals into the Atlantic Ocean. The indigenous name described it well. The German settlers sweetened it somewhat by changing it to Swachaub-*mund*, adding their own word for mouth. With the proclamation of Swakopmund as an independent district in 1896, the present way of pronunciation and spelling came into use.

In 1914, with the beginning of the First World War,

Swakopmund harbour was shelled by British naval cruisers and the town was evacuated inland. In 1915 it was occupied by South African troops, following which all harbour activities were transferred from Swakopmund to Walvis Bay. Many of the central government services ceased to function, businesses closed down, the number of inhabitants diminished and the town became less prosperous. However, the natural potential of Swakopmund as a holiday resort was eventually recognised, and subsequently developed. Today, tourism-related services form a major part of the town's economy.

I'm on the verge of abandoning my search for the Swakopmund railway station before it really begins. Everyone I ask seems to not even be aware that their town has such a thing. How can people not know where their railway station is? Then again, I recall it is not even shown on my city map. Perhaps I should have taken that as a sign that it could be in hiding and that I might have trouble finding such a thing.

A railway station without a railway

When I finally manage to track it down, I see a grand building sitting alone, an island surrounded by nothing but bare ground, so bare in fact that there are not even any railway tracks in the vicinity. A railway station without a railway. Having climbed onto the platform, I hear the sounds of whistling coming from an office somewhere inside. I call out and attract the attention of a man on duty. He is very helpful, but with no train movements to take care of, I wonder just what he has to do here all day. Maybe answer silly questions from people like me. He tells me the entire estate, including the station building is in the process of being demolished to make way for a shopping centre. A shopping centre; at least it's not a casino!

'But what about the train I'm supposed to be catching in the morning?' I ask.

'Oh, it's here already. I'll show you. It's over there beyond that fence.'

Lonely and sad, The Pride of Africa, the world's most luxurious train, is hanging its head in shame in an untidy and dusty industrial estate amidst signs of building construction and the disorder that accompanies such activity.

The morning fog is thick. Cars are lined up end to end along the centre of the street in front of the Dunedin Star Guest House. The end of this long line disappears in the mist. All is quiet, almost eerie. Everyone is at church.

At least, because of yesterday's excursion, if nothing else, I have learnt where to direct the taxi driver; not like some others who later relate their own tales of fronting up to a ghost station with a non-existent railway. The train is waiting alongside a dirt track amidst the clutter of an industrial estate; no platform here. To add an element of class and grandeur to the occasion, a red carpet has been laid over the trackside rocks and dust. In addition to that, stewards are waiting, offering hearty welcomes and glasses of champagne as we arrive to have our names checked off the list.

Speaking of Trains

The train consists of twenty-one carriages accommodating fifty-two passengers. In addition to the two dining cars and their adjacent kitchen cars, there is a mid-train lounge as well as the main feature: the open-air observation car at the rear. We are in the Gouritz suite of car number 3384, being fussed over by a blonde and beautiful stewardess who introduces herself as Doline. She drops in whenever we are absent to make our delightful cubby house neat and tidy once again, and check to see if there is a sufficient supply of beer in the little fridge. Gouritz is a spacious deluxe-double room with wood panelling, Edwardian features, a king-size bed taking up the entire width of the room, down bedding, electric blankets, reverse-cycle air-conditioning, ample storage, full-length wardrobe, full-length mirror, a desk, chairs, safe, and coffee and tea-making facilities. An ensuite bathroom forms part of the accommodation, and everything from toiletries to slippers and dressing gowns is provided. Little gifts appear sporadically: survival packs of biscuits; playing cards; chocolates. This is more than enough to convert a person who says he is not overly-fussed with luxury.

Now, I had never before heard the word Gouritz, and had no idea of what it signified. Thankfully, a plaque on the wall tells the story:

The Gouritz River in the Eastern Cape derives its name from the Gouritwa Koi who frequented the area. Bartholomens Diaz, the fifteenth century Portuguese explorer, is reputed to have landed near the mouth in 1488. This relatively large river by South African standards enjoys another claim to fame in the form of the steel railway bridge crossing it. At sixty-four metres it was the highest bridge on the Cape gauge of three feet, six inches. However, the bridge carrying the two-foot gauge railway over the van Stadens River near Port Elizabeth eclipses it at a height of seventy-seven metres above the waters. In 1897, the Cape Government Railways built three kitchen cars which in 1913 were converted to twelve-seater dining cars. One of these was named Gouritz and it survived until 1956 on the South African Railways.

This is all pretty interesting stuff, but I'm still none the wiser. In any case it is not as exciting as some of the other names given to suites towards the rear of the train. From the passenger list, I see that Rorke's Drift, Isandlwana and other, more famous events from history are in vogue.

This marvellous train is the brainchild (or perhaps the lovechild) of Rohan Vos, a brilliant entrepreneur and rugged individualist who had already accumulated a fortune. With nothing better to do, he decided to run a train into Africa using steam, diesel and electric engines. Many of his fellow Africans shook their heads in wonder, regarding him as mad and his optimistic project as impossible. Now, his exquisite, high-end trains ply various routes around southern Africa. Mr Vos has been heard to declare, 'I may not be as wealthy as I once was, but boy, have I got one hell of a train set.'

As we move away about fifteen minutes behind the scheduled departure time, slums come into view on the eastern edge of the town, shattering my first impressions of how neat and tidy Swakopmund was. In the dust of an arid landscape there are row upon row of shacks. Raggedy children run alongside, cheering and waving as we pass. Then the desert is upon us. Out on the open deck, we gather for drinks: the first of many similar sessions to come. This is the rear of the train supposedly offering sweeping views, but we are being pulled backwards by a dirty, noisy, smelly Trans Nib diesel locomotive. Sweeping views indeed; all is taken up by the untidy rear end of a locomotive.

A call to lunch: a sumptuous affair, a taste of what is in store regarding meals in the dining car. Our first introduction to Pride of Africa cuisine: four petite but delightful courses with matching wines. It is amazing how quickly one can make good friends on such a journey: a couple of Kiwis to exchange the usual friendly insults and banter; several South Africans whose sense of humour almost equals mine; a brace of Poms, Americans and others who all add to the enjoyment of a great adventure. Ultimately we will meet everyone who wants to be met, either at the bar in the lounge or sharing meals in the dining car.

One fellow traveller is Bob, an American from Pennsylvania. He is a funny man with many a good story to relate, including the telling of the exchange with his travel agent back home when, along with several others, he finds himself dumped at the Swakopmund station: no train, not even a railway line.

'She tries to tell me that if I had followed her directions and taken the transfer from the hotel as instructed, instead of deciding to get there by myself, there would have been no trouble,' he says. 'I'm determined to keep my cool as I slowly and methodically explain to her that the transfer mini-bus from the hotel actually followed my taxi to the same deserted spot and also discharged its load of passengers there.'

I enjoy his company and his slow-talking cynicism. We both agree that Amtrak, the American passenger system is good fun and not deserving of the endless criticism it seems to attract. We discuss the merits of such great trains as The City of New Orleans and The Coast Starlight. I ask him if he is married.

'Oh yes, but when I plan these sorts of trips, I always start out by telling her she would not enjoy it.'

Another couple easy to befriend are from Lancashire, elderly and, to our mutual surprise and delight, are on their honeymoon.

Not easy to ignore, another combination comprises a man with an unidentifiable accent and an Australian girl. She is tall and thin and likes to wrap her long legs around those of any bar stool on which she happens to be seated.

Travel is slow, but we are in no hurry to get anywhere. It is the journey that counts, not necessarily the destination. The initial outlay for this trip covers all meals, drinks, off-train excursions, room service and a limited laundry service. I've never before been on a train that offers a laundry as part of the deal. This one also boasts that it has no Wi-Fi (more about this later), nor television, nor radios on board. And, don't even think about bringing laptops or mobile phones into the dining cars or lounges. This is all about providing the epitome of luxury, harking back to a bygone era when train travel was decadent and romantic.

Waking from an afternoon nap, I discover that we are passing through a small town, churches with tall spires, trees and patches of green grass, and mountain ranges on each side turning purple in the setting sun.

Meals, especially dinner, are special events on board this train. Men are required to wear a jacket and tie, with ladies frocking-up for the occasion. An excellent meal and the opportunity to meet more new people, all enhanced by doing so in the confines of a pillared dining car.

We travel through the night. In the darkness, beyond my bedroom (Oops, suite) window I see that we have come to Kranzberg, a junction for lines running north to Tsumeb and south to Windhoek.

Namibia's nasty secret

Beneath the surface of all that is neat and charming in modern day Swakopmund and Windhoek, there lies a dirty side that has been kept hidden from the general public for the past one hundred years. The twentieth century's first-ever efforts at exterminating an entire race of people took place here in Namibia. And, this is the example Hitler referred back to when he established his own genocidal policies in Europe some thirty years later.

With the establishment of their South West African colony, settlers moved in, followed by a military governor who knew little about running a colony and nothing at all about Africa. Major Theodor Leutwein began his term of office by playing off the Nama and Herero tribes against each other. More and more white settlers arrived, pushing tribesmen from their cattle-grazing lands with bribes and dodgy deals. At no time was the German Colonial Administration ever fully in control of Namibia. The period between 1890 and 1908 was marred by numerous conflicts and rebellions as the pre-colonial population vented their anger and rose up against the Germans.

Between 1904 and 1907 during what was known as the Herero Wars, the German Colonial Government undertook a campaign of racial extermination and collective punishment against the original inhabitants. German colonial rule was oppressive; the indigenous cultures were gradually being destroyed. Natives were routinely used as slave labourers and their lands were frequently confiscated and given over to newly-arriving colonists encouraged to settle there. That same land was stocked with cattle stolen from the Hereros and Namas, causing ever-increasing resentment. The Herero were originally a group of cattle herders living in the central-eastern region of German South West Africa. Their leaders repeatedly complained that their womenfolk and girls were being raped by Germans: a crime the German authorities were reluctant to punish. Eventually the area was to be inhabited by German settlers and turned into 'African Germany'. Over the next decade, the land and the cattle, so essential to Herero and Nama lifestyles, passed into the Germans' hands.

Suggestions were being made by the colonial government as to the possibility of establishing native reserves and confining the Herero to them. The gap between the rights of a European and an African was demonstrated by the legal view of the German Colonial League: the testimony of seven Africans equaled that of one white man. The average German colonist regarded native Africans as a lowly source of cheap labour, while other settlers went much further, actually advocating their complete extermination.

In 1903 the Herero became aware of a plan to divide their territory with a railway line, and the establishment of reservations in which they would be concentrated. In that same year, under the leadership of Hendrik Witbooi, some of the Nama tribes rose in revolt. Witbooi had earlier written to Governor Leutwein, complaining on behalf of the native Africans about the invaders who had taken their land and deprived them of their rights to run their own animals on it. There were other issues such as the use of the scanty water supplies and the imposition of alien laws and taxes. Witbooi's hope was that Leutwein would recognise the injustice of what was occurring, offer sympathy and perhaps do something about it.

Rebellion.

A number of factors, the main one being land rights, led the Herero to join the other ethnic group the Nama in January 1904. On 11 January the leader of the Herero, Samuel Maharero ordered the extermination of all white people in the German protectorate, with the exception of the English, Boers, Mamas and missionaries. The following day, several hundred mounted Herero invaded Okahandja. They killed one hundred and twenty-three people, most of them German soldiers and farmers, and set fire to buildings in the town.

By 14 January the violence had spread as far as Omarasa, north of a place called the Waterberg. Post offices were destroyed and the Waterberg military station was occupied. All colonial soldiers stationed there were killed. On 16 January Gobabis was besieged and a German military company was ambushed near Otjiwarongo. Maharero allowed missionaries, along with a small number of German women and children free passage to Okahandja which they reached on 9 April 1904.

By 1903, the Herero had already ceded more than a quarter of their one hundred and thirty thousand square kilometres to German colonists. This was before the railway line running from the Atlantic coast to inland German settlements was constructed. Completion of this line would make the German colonies more accessible, ushering even more Europeans into the area.

A new policy on debt collection, enforced that same year, also played a major role in fostering the uprising. For many years the Herero population had fallen into the trap of borrowing money at extreme interest rates from unscrupulous white traders. As most Hereros had no means of paying back the loans, much of the debt went uncollected and continued to accumulate. In an effort to correct the growing problem, Governor Leutwein decreed, with all good intentions, that debts not repaid by the end of the following year would be voided. To speedily recoup their loans, and in the absence of hard cash, traders often seized cattle or whatever objects of value they could lay their hands on. This generated even more Herero resentment towards the Germans, escalating to hopelessness when they realised the German officials' sympathy lay with the traders who were about to lose what was owed to them.

In the first phase of his solution, Leutwein led the colonial troops and marine reinforcements in a fairly standard campaign that drove the Herero back from the towns and the unfinished but strategic railway. In April 1904 he succeeded in pushing the Herero out of the colony's centre towards a place known as the Waterberg on the edge of the Omaheke desert.

With his troops low on ammunition, Leutwein prudently pulled back, an action interpreted by the distant General Staff as a defeat. The colonel was removed and Lieutenant-General Lothar von Trotha chosen as his replacement. Appointed Supreme Commander of South West Africa on 3 May 1904, he arrived on 11 June with an expeditionary force of fourteen thousand imperial colonial troops. Upon arrival, and intending to pacify the region, he launched into the next phase of the operation: surround the Herero at the Waterberg and defeat them all in a single, pitched battle.

General Trotha made clear his intentions regarding his proposed solution to ending the Herero resistance. In a letter, he wrote: *I believe that the nation as such should be annihilated, or, if this is not possible by tactical measures, have to be expelled from the country ... This will be possible if the water-holes from Grootfontein to Gobabis are occupied. The constant movement of our troops will enable us to find the small groups of nation who have moved backwards and destroy them gradually.*

By this stage, the Herero believed their conflict with the Germans was all over and, under their leader Mahahrero, they were waiting to begin peace negotiations. By the beginning of spring, some eight thousand of them had gathered at the Waterberg, expecting to engage with von Trotha in land rights discussions. Instead, on 11 August, he attacked them by pouring his ill-trained troops into the battle. The Herero warriors, and the entire group of fellow tribes-people who had accompanied them, broke through to the southeast, following the dry riverbeds into the desert. Trotha ordered his few mobile units to pursue the fleeing people, hoping they would turn and give him the opportunity he longed for: to defeat them in another battle. Instead, harassed and fired upon, they struggled farther and farther into the desert. As exhausted Herero fell to the ground, unable to go on, German soldiers, obeying orders, rode up and killed them: men, women and children. All who had fallen into German hands, wounded or otherwise, were mercilessly put to death. The majority of the others died of thirst. German patrols later found skeletons lying around thirteen-metre-deep holes dug in the sand in desperate and vain attempts to find water. It was also claimed that the German colonial army was systematically poisoning the desert wells.

Still under Samuel Mahahrero's leadership, a number of Herero managed to escape the Germans and set out to reach the British territory of Bechuanaland (present day Botswana) in the east, where fewer than one thousand of them were eventually granted asylum. Mahahrero lived there as an exiled leader until his death in 1923.

Those who survived were rounded up by the Germans and placed in concentration camps where they were used as slave labour. The extermination camp at Shark Island also served as a prototype for the Nazi's concentration camps three decades later.

On 2 October General von Trotha issued a warning to the Hereros:

> *I, the great general of the German soldiers, say the Hereros are German subjects no longer. They have killed, stolen, cut off the ears and other parts of the body of wounded soldiers, and now are too cowardly to want to fight any longer. I announce to the people that whoever hands me one of the chiefs shall receive 1,000 marks, and 5,000 marks for the leader Samuel Mahahrero. The Herero nation must now leave the country. If it refuses, I shall compel it to do so with the "long tube" (cannon). Any Herero found inside the German frontier, with*

or without a gun or cattle, will be executed. I shall spare neither women nor children. I shall give the order to drive them away and fire on them. Such are my words to the Herero people.

He issued the following orders to his troops:

This proclamation is to be read to the troops at roll-call, with the addition that the unit that catches a captain will also receive the appropriate reward, and that the shooting at women and children is to be understood as shooting above their heads, so as to force them to run away. I assume absolutely that this proclamation will result in taking no more male prisoners, but will not degenerate into atrocities against women and children. The latter will run away if one shoots at them a couple of times. The troops will remain conscious of the good reputation of the German soldier.

Back home in Germany, the general staff were well aware of the atrocities taking place in their far-off colony. Their official publication *Der Kampf*, noted:

This bold enterprise shows up in the most brilliant light the ruthless energy of the German command in pursuing their beaten enemy. No pains, no sacrifices were spared in eliminating the last remnants of enemy resistance. Like a wounded beast the enemy was tracked down from one water-hole to the next, until finally he became the victim of his own environment. The arid Omaheke Desert was to complete what the German army had begun: the extermination of the Herero nation.

One of the more appalling features of this mass destruction of human lives was the open publicity in which the perpetrators seemed to rejoice. Picture postcards were produced, displaying in particular the concentration camps. The postcards from the German colony, illustrating a deplorable disregard for human suffering, were conveyed as greetings to the colonists' loved ones back home. The same is true of colour pictures showing scenes of prisoners being hanged, or of forced labour scenes representing 'native life' as though this was a normal feature in the lives of the so-called natives. It seemed natural for the Germans to subject the Africans to such inhuman treatment along with the regular application of brute force.

Having a wonderful time; wish you were here.
A postcard back home to Mum

Eye-witness accounts of what was happening were relayed to parts of the outside world by South Africans who had returned to their homes after working for the Germans in the southwest. One who was aware of the situation wrote that it would be more accurate to describe Shark Island not as a concentration camp or work camp, but as an extermination camp or death camp where medical experiments were carried out, and daily executions took place. With the eventual closure of the concentration camps, all surviving Herero were distributed as labourers for the German settlers. From that time on, all Herero over the age of seven were forced to wear a metal disc with their labour registration number displayed on it. They were also banned from owning land or cattle.

German South West Africa was the incubator for hatching the ideas and methods adopted and developed by the Nazis in Eastern Europe. Operating between 1905 and 1907, Shark Island was the twentieth century's first death camp. In 2004 the German government recognised and apologised for the events that had occurred in Namibia so long ago, but has so far ruled out paying financial compensation to the victims' descendants.

In what was known as the Scramble for Africa, territories were claimed and occupied by expansionist European powers, including in this case Germany. But Germany was slow off the mark and managed to grab only a few colonies in Africa and Oceania, all of which turned out to be dismal and costly commercial failures. In nationalist circles, colonies were regarded as being indispensable to proving the home country's status as a world power. Settler ideology envisaged the creation of a 'New Germany'. On the one hand, under such circumstances, any challenge to colonial rule was tantamount to disparaging national honour and prestige. Of course, at the same time, the quest for settlement translated into a sustained drive to expropriate Africans from their lands and from their livestock.

Before leaving Swakopmund I had come across two war memorials located near each other in a pretty little park. One, unveiled on 10 November 1963, is dedicated to those killed in the Second World War. The other, on a much grander scale and more imposing, is the German Marine Memorial, donated to the town in 1908 by marines from Kiel in memory of those who died while helping to defeat the indigenous Hereros. The Marine Memorial is a startling piece of sculpture: a large boulder featuring a life-size marine sprawled dead across one part of it while another marine at the top is holding a rifle.

German marines' monument in Swakopmund

In a way I am surprised to see the monument still standing undamaged and undefaced; the Germans having effectively abandoned the country at the time of the First World War. A plaque at the base of the monument lists the names of those Germans killed in 1904 and 1905 during their slaughter of the Hereros. One critic of this rather morbid monument is recorded as describing the sentiment behind it as follows: 'No doubt those marines were facing little old Herero women armed with sharpened mango slicers.'

I failed to find any memorial to the many native people who were wiped out during the genocide period, nor to the thousands who later perished as prisoners in the concentration camps. It is estimated that about fifteen thousand Hereros survived the annihilation campaign, and some two hundred and fifty thousand still live in Namibia today.

The railway comes to Namibia

The Namib Desert is certainly not the most inviting place in which to build a railway.

Hunter-gatherers who once roamed these bone-dry gravel plains and shifting sands dubbed it 'The land God made in anger'. Early Portuguese mariners who came to grief on its aptly named Skeleton Coast called its hinterland 'The sands of hell'. Nineteenth century Swedish naturalist and explorer, Charles Andersson, recorded his first memorable impression of it, 'A shudder, amounting almost to fear, overcame me when its frightful desolation suddenly broke upon my view. Death would be preferable to banishment in such a country.'

This is the land the Nama people called Namib, meaning 'Plain without end'. It stretches for more than eight hundred kilometres north to south, and one hundred and twenty from the Skeleton Coast to the grasslands of the Kalahari. There is no shade because there are no trees, and no rivers because there is no rain to speak of.

Then along came the German soldiers and settlers. In 1897 they decided it would be a good idea to lay a railway line across the desert. In fact, they had little choice. At the time there were no roads worthy of the name anywhere in German South West Africa; the only way of travelling through it was by ox wagon. Then, an epidemic of rinderpest, an acute viral disease affecting cloven-hoofed animals, wiped out ninety percent of the colony's oxen.

The three hundred and seventy-kilometre *staatsbahn* from Swakopmund to Windhoek was completed between 1897 and 1902. It began running passenger and freight services the same year it was finished. Prior to the beginning of the First World War in 1914, most of the larger centres in the German colony had already been linked to the rail network. Following the signing of the Treaty of Versailles, the South West Africa Rail network was incorporated into that of the Union of South Africa.

Windhoek railway station

Windhoek's beautiful old Cape Dutch-style railway station was constructed by the Germans in 1912 and expanded in 1929 by the South African administration. Standing out the front is a sinister, amour-plated vehicle, the likes of which I had never seen before, that could be quickly dispatched to hot spots during the apartheid troubles.

On the station's upstairs floor is the small but interesting Trans-Namib Transport Museum detailing Namibian transport history, particularly that of the railway. I steadily and happily work my way through the exhibits on display, being annoyed every three seconds (or so it seemed) by the man in charge sneaking along the corridor, sticking his head around a corner and asking if everything is OK. I wonder if he thinks I'm in the process of pinching something.

If there is one regret, it would be that steam locomotives in Namibia puffed their last in 1960. However, at just about every stop along the way, one of the old-timers can be seen sitting on a plinth outside the station collecting rust and bird shit.

Etosha National Park

Through the night we have travelled northwest from Swakopmund to Otjiwarongo, branching off the main line at Kranzberg sometime during the early hours. In the morning we board buses at Otjiwarongo station as the railway between here and the original destination of Tsumeb is undergoing construction, something that has been going on for the past two years or so, as we are told. It is cold.

Without going into details of game drives and being up close with any number of the park's inhabitants, I will relate only an incident that enhanced our anti-German experiences.

Back at the lodge after an enjoyable afternoon, dusty and thirsty, beer is in order. The main bar is closed and I am directed to the swimming pool bar. Great, I think. However, my enthusiasm is dented when I arrive and find the five-metre length of bar frontage blocked by a group of noisy, all-conquering Germans, seated at every available stool closely-packed together, guffawing and oblivious to the line-up behind them trying to attract the barman's attention. They have successfully blocked everyone else's chance of ever being served. Then, adding to the mayhem, in their own huddle at one crowded end, half a dozen American men and women are bamboozling another barman with their loud, insistent and overlapping orders for manhattans, screwdrivers, martinis and other concoctions that no serious, self-respecting drinker would ever give thought to. On the verge of giving up and walking off to the room for a shower, one of the befuddled, over-worked stewards finally spots my plight. In a desperate exchange of hand signals and with me waving a ten-dollar note like a distress signal, a large mug of beer is finally handed to me over the heads of the immovable Teutonic barrier.

Next morning's breakfast is waiting for us in the dining room. No sign of last night's German bar-hounds. Buses are ready to carry us back to Otjiwarongo where the train is waiting. This town featured earlier in our story as the place near where a German military company was ambushed by the Herero rebels on 16 January 1904.

Lunch on board the train as we head south, back to the main line and on to Windhoek. Beyond the window, the views are of Acacia trees and wild scrub. We travel on into the late afternoon.

Sou Soussusvlei

Back at Windhoek, after a quick tour of the town – we had already done ours while waiting to get to Swakopmund – we are driven to the airport where a fleet of light aircraft is waiting to take us on the one-hour flight southwest to Soussusvlei, not far inland from the Atlantic coast. The pilot, looking too young to be in charge of such important cargo, instantly wins me over when he casually tells one of his passengers somewhere down the back, 'Don't worry about it' when she claims her seatbelt doesn't work. An uneventful flight, with no need for the lady with the non-working seatbelt to become alarmed. Our boy aviator sets the Cessna Caravan down in a dusty, rattling landing on a gravel airstrip. We transfer to waiting vehicles for the short drive to the lodge. Since Soussusvlei is possibly Namibia's foremost attraction, much has been done by the authorities to support and facilitate tourism in the region.

Soussusvlei situated inside Namib-Naukluft National Park is a salt and clay pan created by a river that flows every five or ten years. Soussus means either 'Place of no Return' or 'Dead End'; take your pick. Neither of them sounds very inviting. The sand dunes here have an intense reddish colour and are among the highest in the world. The highest of them all, at about three hundred and eighty metres, goes by the impressive name of Big Daddy. Another extra-high dune is known as Big Mama. The names remind me of our very own Big Red near Birdsville back in south west Queensland.

Namibia's higher and more stable dunes here are partially covered with a relatively rich vegetation, mainly watered by a number of underground and ephemeral rivers that seasonally flood the pans. Another source of moisture for the region is the humidity brought in with the daily morning fogs entering the desert from the Atlantic Ocean.

Keetmanshoop and Fish River

In 1886 wealthy German industrialist Johan Keetman, provided funds for a mission station to serve the southern portion of what was then South West Africa. It was built on the banks of the Swartmoder (Black Mud) River, which is usually a dry watercourse but occasionally short, violent floods occur when freak rainstorms deluge the watershed.

The mission was named Keetmanshoop (the hope of Keetman) and managed to flourish in a region marked by local conflict, raids, cattle rustling and bloody vendettas. A substantial stone church built in 1895, and now a museum, dominates the town. Keetmanshoop retains its colonial atmosphere, with many of its buildings designed with thick ceilings to fend off the tremendous heat.

We are now into the sixth day of travel. The railway station here is another fine example of German colonial-style architecture. An old steam engine which has seen better days is sitting out the front.

From Keetmanshoop, still early morning, buses are waiting to carry us away to an unusual site about fourteen kilometres north of the town along another well maintained stretch of highway. The Quiver Tree Forest is a popular tourist attraction, containing about two hundred and fifty specimens of *Aloe dichotoma*, a species of aloe that is also locally known as the quiver tree. Early Bushmen hunters used the pliable bark from the trees' branches to make quivers to hold their arrows. These fascinating trees only begin to flower for the first time when they are twenty to thirty years old. The trees are also known for appearing to be upside down; the leaves look as though they could be the roots. The quiver tree has a long history of beliefs, including if you dig one up you will have diamonds for the rest of your life. But as with such stories, there is always a catch. Because these trees are blessed, nobody is willing to dig them up.

Marian Hulme, the owner of this remarkable place has established the Quiver Tree Forest Rest Camp in the midst of massive rocks and the upside down trees. Adding to the bizarre atmosphere, she has created a feast of junkyard art: figures of people and animals from all manner of discarded materials: farm machinery, motorcycles; beer cans, bits and pieces of rusty steel and anything else that might come to hand.

*Junk art and an 'upside down tree'
at Quiver Tree Forest Rest Camp*

Back to the train for lunch and then more travel as we move on into the afternoon. We pass through Coenbult, a dry, brown landscape, goats and cattle foraging for food. A stop at 'Nowhere Central': nothing but desert on all sides. As desolate as this place looks, I later learn that it actually has a name other than the generic 'Middle of Nowhere': Holoog. Anyway, no matter where we are, the ever-ready buses have reappeared and are waiting to take us on the rough, hour-or-so drive to the massive Fish River Canyon. We travel along a dirt road between lines of flat-topped mountains. In the distance ahead is Spiekleberg Mountain which, so we are informed, was used as a base for heliograph transmissions, using the sun's reflection to relay messages.

Fish River Canyon

The incredible Fish River Canyon, developed predominantly during the pluvial times about five hundred million years ago, is second only to Arizona's Grand Canyon in geological importance. However, it was not created by water erosion alone, but received a considerable boost when the valley floor collapsed due to movements in the earth's crust. This enormous gorge, with a depth of five hundred and fifty metres and a width of up to twenty-seven kilometres, meanders along for some one hundred and sixty kilometres. Although only sixty-five kilometres in length, the Fish River is the longest river in Namibia. It is interesting to note that the canyon is a hundred kilometres longer than the river that formed it.

With all those measurements and dimensions running around in my mind, when we arrive it is a bit of a mystery as to just where this great canyon is; its vertical drop is out of view from the flat, dry plateau. The buses park at a substantial rest stop with plenty of benches and picnic tables. A short walk over stony ground brings us to the very edge of the five hundred-metre sheer drop. Whoops! Take an urgent step back.

Back at the rest stop, it is no surprise to find the train staff have set up a bar with huge eskies full of beer and wine. I feel I could almost recoup my initial monetary outlay for this trip in the beer that is being forced upon me. After a while, most of us are reluctant to move, quite happy to be sitting here in the great silence which, along with the sun, has descended upon us, and drinking until the darkness is complete. Full of good cheer, we set off into the blackness in search of The Pride of Africa, hopefully still waiting for us out there somewhere in the night. When her lights finally come into view, they are greeted as a welcome sight. The drinking session back at the amazing canyon has caused a slight delay in the dinner plans. Don't blame me; it wasn't all my fault! But to keep the chefs onside, we have been granted a casual night, no need to dress for dinner tonight. Of course, it is always pleasant to put on the finery and frock-up, but by the same token, it can also be a bit of a relief when we realise we don't have to.

During the night we pass through border control, moving effortlessly from Namibia into the Republic of South Africa and have now stopped at the town of Upington.

Upington and the Wi-Fi thief

It is here that our resident Mr Importance and his partner, both in skimpy shorts and tight T-shirts, decide to show off by jogging purposefully along the edge of the platform, on view to the rest of us through the train's windows. By now, we have just about worked him out and, unimpressed, are becoming fed up with his superior, look-at-me attitude.

This town, on the banks of the Orange River, was named in honour of Sir Thomas Upington the Cape's attorney general. Sir Thomas was the man mainly responsible for bringing peace to the region by liquidating the activities of a gang known as the Orange River Pirates who operated around here. He captured their leader Klaas Lucas and, in 1884 successfully chased the remaining desperadoes away from the place.

In 1890 the missionary Christiaan Schroder installed a pump on the banks of the river and established a pontoon ferry. Along the river banks there are signs of considerable agricultural activity. The region is a centre of fruit, vegetable and cotton production, along with sheep, goats and cattle, as well as a thriving wine industry: a far cry from the desert we have recently ventured through.

A walk around town and a visit to the nearby cemetery to check on a group of isolated headstones I can see tucked away in a lonely corner. As suspected, they turn out to be the graves of South African soldiers killed in both World Wars.

Back on board, train manager Anton tells us there will be a limited amount of Wi-Fi available for those passengers who might want to contact their grandchildren, or make similar essential connections to the outside world. However, by the time I collect my IPad from the suite and attempt to log on, whatever Internet supply there once may have been, is well and truly exhausted.

Underway again at noon, the train crosses a bridge more than one and a half kilometres long, the second longest in South Africa. Grain silos stand tall beside the river. An overhead bridge, so rusted that it looks to be on the verge of disintegration, derelict machinery and old railway equipment surrounded by barbed wire fences, stacks of concrete sleepers in rusting wagons. For a long time we run alongside a strip of white-dirt road. We pass lonely homesteads. Patches of white daisies add their own touch of brightness to the adjacent fields. A water tank and stand-pipe left over from the steam-age. The skeletons of abandoned houses, no signs of life.

Mr Importance and his involvement in that day's Wi-Fi shortage comes to light when I later overhear him in the observation car lounge complaining to Bob the friendly American.

'I could only email five pages of a crucial business report back to head office,' he whines.

Bob tells him to get over it. 'So, what's your problem?' he says. 'Money isn't everything. I'm pretty sure the sun will rise in the east again tomorrow. And, if it was so important, why were you doing it out here in the middle of the bloody Kalahari Desert?'

But by eavesdropping on this conversation, I realise that this overly self-important fool had stolen the entire ration of cyber space that should have been shared amongst the rest of us. If he had shut up about it and not turned it into his very-own major crisis, seeking sympathy from someone, anyone, none of us would ever have been the wiser. From then on, we all become aware of his selfishness, mainly because I have taken it upon myself to tell others who were disappointed at being unable to make their own contact. Antagonism then turns to his partner: guilt by association.

'An Australian skank', is one uncomplimentary description I hear being bandied about.

Oh dear, what have I started?

Dissention within the ranks.

Kimberley

The story of Kimberley is the story of diamonds. The romantic associations of De Beers, Cecil John Rhodes and the Cape to Cairo Railway are all centred here.

The train finally arrives in Kimberley after a pause at De Ar: a Dutch word meaning artery, referring to an underground watercourse running through the area. The name was originally bestowed on a farm which, because of its ideal location, was bought by the government in 1881, allowing the first railway line from Cape Town to Kimberley to be built.

Along the way we see conical-shaped hills in the distance, and pass homesteads sitting amid their own patches of green grass, windmills and sheep. In the front yard of one of the houses, a black woman is doing the laundry in a washtub out in the garden.

Belmont station. From here on, the line is electrified. There are silos and rusty overhead bridges. Witput siding. Stacks of concrete sleepers. Belmont. The train is reversed here to make a backwards entry into Kimberley. From here on, the line is electrified.

When we spot a mob of feral horses, I tell my African friend that in Australia we call them brumbies. His eyes light up in recognition.

'That answers the question of where the Canberra rugby

union team's name comes from. A bunch of wild horses,' he says. 'Well, there you go. It is true that you learn something every day.'

Diamonds had been discovered near Hopetown in 1867, but it was the discovery in 1871 of a 'diamond pipe' where the massive Big Hole now plunges towards the centre of the earth which triggered the great Diamond Rush. The Big Hole, beginning as a small hill, was flattened and slowly became an enormous hole from where millions of tonnes of diamondiferous blue-ground Kimberlite ore have been removed. It is now the largest man-made hole in the world where underground workings were once carried out at a depth of more than a kilometre.

Literally thousands of claims were pegged out as would-be miners from all corners of the world joined the rush, seeking to make their fortunes. As the ore was removed, the diggers continued their search hundreds of metres below ground level. With some diggers working faster than others, those still at the higher levels caused mud and gravel to be washed down into the lower claims during summer cloudbursts. As the hole became deeper, water pooled in the base and it became necessary to have it pumped out.

Into the midst of this competitive chaos emerged two men, wildly different in background, education and personality: Barney Barnato and Cecil John Rhodes. Both men had a similar vision and forcefully stamped their respective ideals on early Kimberley. Barnato took control of the Kimberley Central Mine, while Rhodes assumed control of the De Beers Mine where the Big Hole is located. Both men agreed that the supply of diamonds to the world market had to be regulated through the formation of a monopoly or cartel. The question was, which one would buy out the other? In 1888, after intense negotiations, De Beers bought out Barnato, then promptly appointed him Life Governor of the new De Beers Consolidated Diamond Mines.

Once De Beers had taken complete control of the diamond industry, Kimberley went from a wild, raucous town of young male miners to a company town where the tide of wealth ebbed away, never to return. It gradually settled down to producing its own diamonds and later to sorting and cutting diamonds from all over the world.

In addition to its stories of diamonds and the Big Hole, Kimberley has another fascinating tale to tell. During the Boer War, the town was besieged while Cecil Rhodes was still resident inside. The British Army, under Lord Methuen attempted to relieve the town but suffered two serious setbacks: at the battles of Modder River on 28 November 1899 and Magersfontein on 11 December 1899. Kimberley was only relieved two months later after a great cavalry dash across the Karoo led by Sir John French and Colonel Douglas Haig: both of whom went on to achieve further fame in the Great War.

At the beginning of the siege the artillery defence of Kimberley consisted of just seven pairs of two-point-five-inch muzzle-loading rifles. The idea of manufacturing a gun that could outrange the Boer artillery is credited to an American engineer named George Labram who had come to South Africa in 1893 to install a crusher plant at one of the Kimberley mines. He was eventually appointed De Beers' Chief Engineer. Labram designed and manufactured the weapon, a four-point-one-inch rifled breech loading gun which was to become known as the Long Cecil Gun in honour of Cecil Rhodes.

During the first three weeks of the siege Labram also designed and constructed a plant for the bulk refrigeration of perishable food items; essential in a location with such high summer temperatures. In addition to that, he installed an emergency fresh water supply system which, apart from one or two wells around the place, became the town's water source for the duration of the siege.

*Engineer George Labram (second from right)
with Long Cecil*

By the end of November the garrison's artillery had expended almost one third of its ammunition. Labram converted part of De Beers' workshops over to making shells, charges and fuses for the two-point-five-inch guns, never before having had anything to do with gun-making.

The Long Cecil Gun was designed and constructed by engineers who also had no previous experience of ordnance manufacture. They worked from descriptions they found in a stray copy of an old engineering manual. From the day that designs were fashioned and completed, it took just twenty-four days to construct the gun. On 19 January 1900 it was taken for testing and calibration at one of the three emplacements that had been prepared in advance. Rhodes, who had taken a great interest in the gun and its manufacture was present, along with a number of local dignitaries and senior military officers. The first round fired in anger from Long Cecil landed some seven thousand metres away smack bang in the middle of a hitherto safe and quiet Boer laager, causing 'considerably alarm and dismay' according to Boer letters written at the time and later intercepted by the British.

During its active life, Long Cecil fired off two hundred and twenty-five shells against the enemy at an average range of five thousand metres. Its impact on the Boers forced them to send for one of their own Long Tom Guns. Ironically, Labram was killed by one of the first shells this same gun fired into Kimberley. Long Cecil is on display in Kimberley where it stands as a memorial to those who defended the town during the siege.

The Kimberley Mine Museum can lay claim to being one of the most impressive museums in all of South Africa, encompassing the whole area of the Big Hole. Out in the open are many of the original corrugated-iron buildings and tools used by the original miners. There are restored vintage trams and derelict, unloved steam locos. The place tells the story of the diamond industry which, prior to the discovery of diamonds in the Northern Cape in 1867, was based in India and Ceylon. Although there are coffee shops and many souvenir outlets within the complex, I see no places offering free samples of the main product.

And it is here at Kimberley that our notorious Wi-Fi thief, and exceedingly important fellow traveller, brings further attention to himself. The rest of us are happily investigating the world's deepest man-made hole and absorbing the history of this once-massive diamond mine. It becomes time to leave and we head out to where the buses are waiting to take us back to the train. Then, at a steady walk, pushing against the tide, and waving his IPad to all and sundry, he announces loudly, 'They've got Wi-Fi, they've got Wi-Fi.' As though any of us cared! He has obviously spent all this time preparing another essential report instead of inspecting an amazing piece of history. By now we are all wishing his bloody essential business reports would choke him.

Underway again. Seventy kilometres north of Kimberley, we cross the Vaal River via a multi-arched bridge. Down to the left, resting in the series of lagoons beside the river are thousands of flamingos. With help from the setting sun, reflections coming off the beautiful birds are colouring the water pink and purple. A glorious sight, and certainly a fitting finale to a wonderful journey.

The final night. Drinks on the rear deck. Reluctant to leave, unwilling to tear ourselves away to dress for dinner. A farewell gala affair with our stewards and stewardesses dressed in formal wear and our own Doline more gorgeous than ever in her evening gown. The party looks set to continue into the night, but with my raging days well and truly behind me, I opt for bed.

In the morning amidst the hangovers and stray balloons and streamers lingering from the previous night's frivolities, our train is making a high-speed dash as though it can't wait to get home. Suburbs, commuter stations and a vast network of railway. President Station and Germiston Station. Packed with workers, electric trains buzz back and forth around us. At every station, the platforms are jammed with black people; these are not places for white businessmen dressed in three-piece suits and clutching brief cases.

Hiding in a side track is Tiffany the steam engine. She sidles up to escort us on the final leg of our trip. After many years of regular service, dating back to 1893, this engine was cosmetically restored and placed on display at Winburg station in the Free State. When Rohan Vos spotted her during one of his travels, it was love at first sight. He purchased the locomotive in 1987 and began the task of returning her to the rails. She is believed to be one of the oldest working steam engines in the world. As with all his other engines, she is named after a member of the Vos family. If anyone is puzzled over the origin of the name King Zog being bestowed on one of them, the answer lies in the fact that it is named after the family's faithful Dalmatian.

Tiffany slips in behind us

The appearance of a massive university wrapped around a hillside brings recognition to our African friends along with the knowledge that there is not much further to go. With Tiffany hissing and huffing behind us, we glide through the suburbs of Pretoria and pull in to the private railway station at Capital Park. This once bustling centre of steam locomotion in the old Transvaal is now Rovos Rail's headquarters. We have covered just on three thousand kilometres of train travel; time for farewells, and promises to keep in touch, invariably never kept, and a search for our luggage amongst the pile dumped in the waiting room. No sign of the person who stole our Wi-Fi allocation, nor his lanky partner. I can only assume they are off somewhere, huddled in a corner, busily preparing another essential business report.

Arrival at this gracious colonial-style terminus in the nation's administrative capital might signal the end of one train journey, but not the end of my stories.

Chapter Two: The Hudson Bay

As The Hudson Bay left Winnipeg station at ten o'clock on a bitterly cold night, there was only a smattering of passengers in the sitting car I'd boarded. The conductor said, 'Spread yourselves out, there's plenty of room.' The one thousand, six hundred and ninety-seven-kilometre, two-night side trip began with a run back into Saskatchewan where the tracks would leave the main transcontinental line and sweep away to the north before re-entering Manitoba early next morning.

My first sight beyond the window on that new day was of more grain wagons and a tall elevator, painted red with the name Pioneer written along its side. Powdery snow flew back like dust on either side of the train. We passed through forests of spruce trees hung heavy with snow and crossed over little streams of black water that were gradually turning to ice along their edges. The snow on the ground became thicker as the train approached The Pas where there was a long stop to take on water and refuel the twin locomotives.

The Pas was a big town sitting in isolation in a snow-covered wilderness. I had expected to see a settlement about the size of Thallon in southern Queensland, but was surprised to notice the familiar red and white stripes of a KFC restaurant, a number of four-storeyed buildings, a church with a tall steeple, and in a park, a monument that looked like a war memorial with several frost-shrouded wreaths propped against its base. Children laughed and played amongst the snow in the grounds of a schoolyard across from the station.

The conductor, ever informative, said, 'A bit further on, you'll see the mileposts on the right hand side of the train. I'll just explain what's going on with them. They start at zero from The Pas. Further along we'll be branching off to go into Thompson and then turn around and come back out to the main line again.'

We passed a big lake on the right hand side that had little waves rippling across its surface. Farther on there was the settlement of Cormorant clinging to the edge of Lake Wekucko. We linked up with a highway running towards the town of Thompson, then paused for a while at Wabowden where the Silver Leaf Hotel, directly across from the station, had several pickup trucks nosed into the front of the building.

The sun came out as we passed our southbound counterpart at 3.20 in the afternoon.

An American man, letting everyone within earshot know he came from California, and bearing a frightening resemblance to the character in the 'Waldorf Salad' episode of the Fawlty Towers television comedy, sat in a seat across the aisle from me. He was so loud and overbearing that I silently nicknamed him 'Pita' (Pain In The Arse). He seemed under some obligation to regale me with a story about a cousin's RV (recreational vehicle, or caravan as we would call it) adventure driving around Australia. I soon lost the thread of what he was saying as it dawned on me that the telling of this tale was going to take longer than the actual trip. When he lunged at a passing conductor and bullied him into selling an upgrade to a sleeper, I was not sorry to see him leave. However, I marvelled at how easy it had been for him to get a sleeper when I had been told earlier back in Winnipeg there were none available on this section of the trip; I'd been able to get one for the return leg only. I thought of asking the conductor if there was another sleeper available for me, but then decided against it, reasoning that I would sooner suffer another night in the sitter coach than be subjected to Pita in the sleepers. What if I had to share one with him?

Later in the afternoon a short man in a thick shirt of lumberjack tartan, jeans and heavy boots, and with his hair pulled back into a stringy ponytail staggered through the door. Until then I had been the sole occupant of the partitioned-off section of the dining car that served as a lounge area. I was writing up my diary at one of the four tables when the man sat down opposite me, leaned across the table and looked up into my eyes. He pushed a soggy container of chips and gravy towards me, motioning for me to help myself. When I shook my head 'No', he mumbled a string of words that, apart from a clearly audible 'beer', were unintelligible. I thought he was asking me to buy him a drink, but he then produced a can from somewhere within his tatty clothes and offered one to me.

'No, no, no,' I pleaded. 'No thanks.'

His gaze turned to disbelief and his mouth, crowded with twisted teeth and dangling, half-chewed chips, hung open like a rusty trap. I tried to ignore him, hoping desperately that he wasn't dangerous and that I hadn't offended him. He gave up on me after a while and moved to a corner chair where, when I chanced a furtive glance, I saw that he had fallen asleep. Half an hour later, the conductor arrived and gently shook him awake.

'Come on, Eddie. Time to get off.'

Eddie stumbled back through the door. He was obviously one of the train's 'regulars' and hadn't been dangerous at all. He got out at Thicket Portage, a muddy little town with a yellow wooden church – St Josepheus Catholic Church – perched on the side of a hill. I felt ashamed then that I'd not been a little more tolerant towards him. Too late I realised he had meant no harm and would probably have welcomed and appreciated a gesture of friendship.

The train turned left at the two hundred-mile post exactly as the conductor had said it would and headed west towards Thompson. As we moved closer to this long-awaited destination, the sun began to set over the lakes and forests. The train did a U-turn around a triangle and reversed into Thompson station at 6.00 pm – one hour late. Some quick-thinking passengers, obviously well in the know, had arranged for a pizza delivery to be ready and waiting as we pulled up.

In the station waiting room there was a newspaper dispenser with instructions and costs – one looney, two quarters – written on it for obtaining the Saturday paper. The Canadian one dollar coin had received the nickname 'looney' because of the duck, known locally as a looney bird featured on its reverse side. By extension, the two dollar coin was known as a 'tooney'.

I settled in for one more night in my seat in the coach class carriage, grateful that I would not have to suffer Pita's chatter again. By then the car was beginning to resemble a teenager's bedroom. It was littered with rubbish and clothing and bodies strewn at awkward angles along its length.

In the darkness beyond the train window, I could see the telegraph poles that lurched at ever-varying angles beside the line. Some of the posts were propped up in a triangular frame that must have provided maximum support in the frigid Arctic conditions. Sometimes the posts were lying on the ground, sometimes they were leaning at such an angle that the wires were tangled in bushes or hanging in loops in the snow.

Telegraph poles, I thought. What a lovely old description, one that just seems to linger on as part of railway lore – I'm sure it had been many years since anything had been 'telegraphed' over those lines.

We arrived at Churchill early the following morning to heavy snow and a howling wind. Whatever the minus something-or-other temperature was, it was being dragged even lower by a vicious wind-chill factor. Beyond the window of the little railway station, visibility was about thirty metres. Everyone on the train, apart from me, seemed to know what they were doing and where they were heading. The entire load of passengers soon disappeared into the fleets of waiting buses and package-tour vehicles. Within fifteen minutes I was the only person left in the building.

I asked the young girl, the solitary staff member at the station, what people did in Churchill until the train departed later that day. She was most helpful; I'm sure she'd been asked the same question many times before. She passed me a hand-drawn map of the town and pointed me in the direction of Gypsy's Bakery. 'They'll look after you,' she said.

Churchill railway station

I battled the wind and slipped and slid over the ice-covered roadway, all the while remaining conscious of the fact that it wouldn't be too hard to miss the place and just keep on going and becoming hopelessly lost in the limited visibility. I had visions of myself steadily staggering off into the wilderness, blissfully unaware that I'd overshot the end of the street, then being devoured by a polar bear.

Gypsy's Bakery, Pastry & Coffee Shop was a low-set, dark red building that had the appearance of a suburban panel beater's shop. Snow was piled around the base of the walls and against the entrance door that led into a little alcove where patrons were able to stamp the snow from their boots as they began the process of shedding layers of clothing. Through another door and I was in a genuine sanctuary. Men with hands wrapped around big mugs of coffee sat at tables, leaning towards each other in the way people do when they indulge in serious gossip. I noticed a distinct lull in the conversation as I entered and felt all eyes turning to check out the stranger in town. I ordered coffee and toast, and sat at a corner table in the warmth of the bakery, taking time to thaw out and to write some letters and postcards.

I later sought refuge in a large building known as the Town Centre Complex and for a happy half-hour watched a group of schoolboys practicing ice hockey. As I watched the bewildering chaos I was reminded of the American sports announcer who said he once went to an all-in brawl that erupted into an ice hockey game. The complex also housed a high school, a health centre and a library, and was the venue for town council meetings. The minutes and agenda items were posted on a notice board, and I spent an enjoyable half hour reading about the shortage of funds available for road maintenance, new garbage collection arrangements that were about to be initiated, and the need for polar bear alert drills at the school.

Pinned to another board were newspaper clippings expressing concern over an increase in international marine insurance charges for users of the Port of Churchill. I read of claims that the increases would needlessly penalise ships using the port. The higher premiums had been assessed because of unfounded fears that ice conditions in Hudson Bay and Hudson Strait would be unsafe by late summer. The article claimed that, after mid-October, oceangoing vessels with no special ice protection would have to pay up to six dollars a tonne more for their insurance to use the port. A ship carrying forty thousand tonnes of grain could expect to pay an extra two hundred and forty thousand dollars in insurance costs. The extra premiums were to be charged even though ships could easily access the port until early November.

The notice described this year's premium hike as 'especially galling' because a mild autumn had left the bay completely ice-free. The policy used by the insurance people directly contradicted Canada's own regulations and guidelines for Arctic Ocean traffic. The federal government provided ice guidelines for Arctic waters that allowed non-ice class vessels to traverse Hudson Bay and the Strait until 5 November each year.

It was interesting stuff. The president of the Hudson Bay Port Company added his comments: *Forcing up insurance rates late in the shipping season was a hoax that has been perpetrated on shippers for decades. The ice in Hudson Bay never freezes into a solid mass because of the natural currents. There hasn't been an iceberg in the bay for probably eight hundred years. The currents in the straits are so strong they don't let icebergs into the bay.*

Mooching around the library I idled past two women, deep in talk. Without meaning to eavesdrop, I caught the tail end of their earnest conversation, 'Ah, the poor thing. She was dying of cancer, you know. And the children were going to be repossessed by Children's Aid.'

The Eskimo Museum, a couple of doors farther along the street beyond the Royal Canadian Mounted Police station, was open. It was warm inside and I found myself to be the sole patron; every other visitor to Churchill was obviously still out on the tundra buggies annoying the polar bears. The museum dated back to 1944 when Roman Catholic missionaries from the order of Oblates of Mary Immaculate saw the need to preserve the carvings and other artefacts representing the culture of the people of the North. In addition to the Inuit artwork, there was also a stuffed polar bear and a wooden chair that once belonged to the explorer Roald Amundsen.

I had with me the letters and cards I'd written earlier at the bakery, and decided to mail them back to Australia. Making general conversation more than any need to actually know the answer, I asked the lady in the post office next door to the museum if they would be going back on the train to Winnipeg with me that night.

'No, you're in plenty of time,' she said. 'They'll make the daily two o'clock plane.'

'What, in this weather?' I must have looked half aghast.

She gaped at me. Her expression asking what's wrong with this bloke? 'Yeah, this is just normal weather for this time of year.'

I battled the blizzard back to Gypsy's Bakery seeking more warmth, a slice of pizza and a mug of hot chocolate. I stayed as long as seemed decent, although the jovial owner told me I was welcome to stay as long as I wanted. He was obviously used to travellers seeking refuge from the cold until their train was due to head south again. On the way back to the station I came across the town's little supermarket and bought a tube of toothpaste and a bottle of water. Then, reasoning that I'd seen all there was to see of Churchill, braved the cold once more and made for the station.

Darkness came down as suddenly as if a curtain had been drawn across a window, the cold increased and the wind took on a demonic moaning sound. The only warm spot in the entire building was the men's toilet where a rattling radiator gave off a thin, wispy heat. The few of us who had arrived early huddled around its doorway, hoping that nobody needed to make urgent use of the place. The building slowly started to fill up as people arrived back from their day's adventure in the tundra buggies, stamping snow from their boots and outdoing each other in their tales of the polar bears they had seen out on the ice. I could see no trace of Pita. Perhaps the entire complement of a tundra buggy had decided they'd had enough and fed him to one of the bears.

The train had been sitting patiently all day in front of the station. However, before we were allowed on board, it had to go through a procedure that was obviously a railroading ritual in this part of the world. We were warned in direct terms to stand well clear, in fact to not even venture out onto the platform.

The train suddenly lurched forward, screeched to an awkward halt after only a few metres and charged backwards to its starting spot. Splinters of ice flew through the air. After a few more jerky backwards and forwards movements, it sat still. As I watched through the window I realised why we had been warned to stay away. Because it had been standing out in below-freezing temperature all day, its wheels had frozen to the tracks and had to be snapped free before it could get moving again.

We were allowed to board at 9.30, and I crawled straight into my allocated bunk behind the set of heavy curtains that offered a modicum of privacy. I was reminded of the famous scene from the 1959 movie *Some Like It Hot*, although I had no Marilyn Monroe look-a-like to share it with. I lay quietly in the dark, grateful for the warmth and desperately seeking sleep. A group of women in neighbouring bunks up and down the corridor began to move in, calling out to each other as they did so. One of them, with no reason to know that I was ensconced nearby in my little retreat, called to her companions, 'I'm glad there's no men in here. I can use the gents' toilet.'

I was quite happy to let the comment go, not wanting to disillusion them. And I would have done so except that the whole group who, gathering from snippets of their more serious conversation, appeared to be university tutors on some expedition, began to call 'Good night' to each other. It was a scene straight out of *The Waltons*. After the fifth 'Good night, Margaret, Shirley, whoever', I could take no more. In my gruffest voice I countered with a surly 'Good night, Cyril.'

Silence!

Next morning we waited for another train, this one headed by two green and gold locomotives of the Hudson's Bay Railway, to come off the Thompson line before ours could enter the triangle allowing it to turn and reverse into the station. However, halfway through the exercise, somebody had a change of mind and the train did another slow circuit of the formation, straightened up and headed in engine first. The carload of talkative women who, after a couple of sheepish looks (from me as well as them), smiled and forgave me my prank from last night, gathered their luggage about them and made ready to leave the train.

We departed on time and at 1.40 pm were back at Thompson Junction ready to link up with the main line again. The simplicity and sparseness of the infrastructure belied the junction's importance. All there was to the place was a tin shed and a toilet with its door hanging open and leaning to one side on only one hinge. Propped against a wall were a broom and a shovel to keep the points free of snow. One of the engineers hopped down from the leading locomotive, did what was necessary with the points to get the train back onto the main north-south line then swung up into the last car as it went past him, and walked back through the train to his position up front.

We were soon back at Thicket Portage – I recognised the beautiful St Josepheus Catholic Church on a slight rise near the tracks. I kept a special eye out in case Eddie was about to board again, thinking that this time I might be a little more pleasant and civil towards him, but he didn't show. The town also had a miniature baseball pitch whose empty wooden stands rose in a vee-shape behind the batter's plate. There were a couple of log cabins and a shop with the words 'Bignell's Store' written above the door.

We moved on through forests of spruce, silver birch, aspen and poplar trees all of which had snow clinging to their branches. At 3.20 pm at Lyddal we passed a northbound Hudson Bay. At the tiny settlement of Wabowden an extra twenty kilometres down the track, I saw another beautiful little wooden church, this one painted green and white.

While ordering dinner in the dining car, I overheard some of the crew members radioing ahead for pizzas to be delivered to the train when we arrived at The Pas. I wished then that I'd been in the know, that I'd remembered the procedure from the previous time. Perhaps I could have invited myself into the group. I felt envious as I listened to their chatter: 'What do you want on yours? Pan fried? Do you want thick or crispy thin?'

'Hold the anchovies.'

We pulled into The Pas while I was sitting at a table with two young Korean girls. They were both very pretty, shy and polite, and told me they were students taking time off from their studies to travel through Canada. I must have created a good impression with them because they asked the steward to take a photograph of the three of us eating dinner together.

Finishing the meal I stepped down into the snow and the cold Arctic night. Everyone on the platform was looking up towards the heavens. Following their gaze I saw the Aurora Borealis dancing and waving across the dark sky like velvet curtains of green and yellow. My side trip into the Arctic wilderness had paid off in a spectacular way; this was a dividend I'd not even given thought to when I decided to make the trip to Churchill and back. The Northern Lights, according to Inuit legend, are spirits of deceased ancestors playing soccer in the sky. The story goes that if you whistle, the lights will swoop down upon you. If you rub your fingernails together quickly they will return to the heavens. Although I love a good legend I had to give some thought as to how long the game of soccer had played such an important part in ancient Eskimo history.

Early morning found The Hudson Bay back in Portage la Prairie. The conductor began stripping the linen from the bunks and loosely piling it into a heap near the door. He told me the outside temperature was minus ten degrees. We pulled into Winnipeg at 8.00 am, leaving me with seven hours to fill in before the next eastbound Canadian was due to arrive and take me on to Toronto.

I was just in time to become caught up in a wedding party which, in a noisy bundle, had tumbled into the foyer of the station to have photographs taken. They lined up for a series of artistic shots in the centre of the concourse where rays of sunlight trickled down upon them through the dust particles. It was entertaining stuff, the fun of it all was becoming contagious. A small crowd soon gathered to watch the antics. When the photographer ran up the stairs to the balcony to take some shots from above, he was chased by a security guard, determined to put a dampener on the proceedings.

'You need permission to come up here,' we heard the security man say.

'I've got permission,' the photographer countered.

A running argument then developed with the photographer keeping one jump ahead of the security man who, in an instant, had become the villain of the piece. The photographer did what he wanted, including one energetic shot where he had the wedding party – on the count of three – leaping off the floor and throwing their arms into the air.

As he came back down the stairs the audience, now formed in a circle around the happy group, was on the verge of booing the evil security man.

'Miserable old git,' one matronly lady said to him.

Chapter Three:
Riding a Typhoon in Vietnam

It had been many years since my first visit to Hanoi when I'd arrived there by train from Beijing. This time I was approaching the Vietnamese capital from the south. And, once again, I was doing it by train.

From Ho Chi Minh City, or Saigon as everyone still calls the place, in southern Vietnam, a metre-gauge railway line runs for one thousand, seven hundred and twenty-six kilometres to Hanoi. A bit of research before I left home threw up some interesting facts. The line is intersected by many roads in any number of populated areas along its length and collisions between trains and vehicles are frequent. The railway was constructed during the time of the French colonists as part of a rail network throughout French Indochina. The Hanoi-Saigon Railway line was officially inaugurated on 2 October 1936. In 1954, following the Geneva Accords, Vietnam was divided into two parts: the communist North and the anti-communist South. During the Vietnam War, the line was subjected to bombardment by the armies of both North and South Vietnam. Following the fall of Saigon on 30 April 1975, the country was united, as was the railway. Vietnam's war-torn railway was fully restored and put back into operation on 31 December 1976.

I had arrived in Saigon several days earlier, travelling by boat down the Mekong River from Cambodia. With no trouble, I was able to engage a local tour company to buy train tickets for me and to show me around the city. This was all done smoothly and efficiently with no hint of the disruptions to come.

The whole world (with the exception of this particular company) was aware that a typhoon was on its way, about to slam into central Vietnam, but let's not worry about that just yet. The man who collected me from the Tan My Dinh Hotel introduced himself as Mr Ky. He was determined I was going to see everything on his itinerary. Although the Vietnam War ended several decades ago, its scars are still visible, mainly because they have now become the country's major tourist attraction.

The Independence Palace, renamed Reunification Palace, was the residence of the President of South Vietnam until the end of the war in 1975. The long struggle for the reunification of Vietnam and the end of foreign intervention in the country's internal politics ended when Chinese-made T-54 tanks smashed through the palace gates. Some of the tanks involved in the historic event were preserved in the palace grounds.

Inside the palace itself, most of its interior was preserved as it was in the 1970s. A UH-1H Huey helicopter sat on the roof, a reminder of those frantic days when United States' helicopters snatched Americans from surrounding rooftops to carry them to waiting navy ships. In the palace basement, the South Vietnamese President's war room was still complete with maps, communication equipment and living quarters.

Just a block behind the Reunification Palace was the War Remnants Museum. From the roadway it looked like a car wrecker's yard with a difference; this one was littered with aircraft and other left-over war pieces. When the museum opened in September 1975 it boasted the unwieldy title of the House for Displaying War Crimes of American Imperialism and the Puppet Government of South Vietnam. Later it was known as the Museum of American War Crimes. Then in yet another name change, it became the War Crimes Museum. In 1993, in line with liberalisation in Vietnam and the normalisation of relations with the United States, it adopted its current name.

One of the buildings in the courtyard is a reproduction of the infamous tiger cages in which the South Vietnamese Government housed political prisoners. Con Son Island, the largest island of the Con Dao archipelago off the coast of southern Vietnam, was infamous during the times of French Indochina. For it was there in 1861 that the French colonial government established a prison to incarcerate political prisoners. In 1954, following the French defeat at Dien Bien Phu, it was turned over to the South Vietnamese Government who continued to use it for the same purpose.

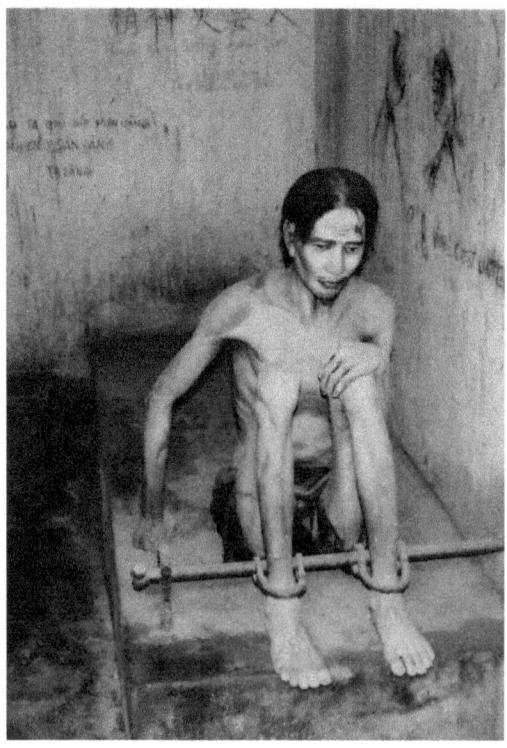

A Vietnamese prisoner

During the Vietnam War, prisoners who'd been held at the prison told of how they'd been abused and tortured during their imprisonment. In July 1970 a United States Congressional delegation visited the prison on what was meant to be a conducted tour. However, guided by a map drawn by a former detainee, two visitors went off on their own. The map led them to a door which was opened from the inside by a guard when he heard them talking outside. Inside they found prisoners shackled within cramped 'tiger cages'. They were covered in sores and bruises, and some were mutilated; they cried out for water when the delegation entered. The re-creation of this horror was so life-like that I jumped back, startled, when I came upon the emaciated figure of a prisoner chained to an iron bar.

My train for the north was originally due to leave at three o'clock, which would have allowed plenty of time for an early morning inspection of the Cu Chi Tunnels, the underground network constructed by Vietnamese fighters during their struggle for independence, and later used as a military base for the Vietcong during the American War. However, advice that the train was now departing at twenty past twelve meant the tunnels visit would have to be forsaken. A disappointed Mr Ky suggested I should remain in Saigon for an extra day so we could go to the tunnels. Although I felt sorry for him in his enthusiasm to show me as much as he could cram in on such a short visit, I decided to stick to my original plan.

To the railway station to board train SDE6. Public address announcements on not what to carry on board the train caused me to wonder just what I was letting myself in for and what sort of people my fellow passengers were. Included among the items forbidden to be brought on board were human corpses and body parts.

I found my way to a four-berth compartment; its dull grey colour scheme reminiscent of a prison cell. The packs of marauding mosquitoes did nothing to cheer me or brighten my sparse confines. The pillow cases on each bunk had little teddy bear designs on them; perhaps they had been purloined from a children's nursery. I waited with dread to see who was going to be sharing my little room with me. A large group of noisy French men and women entered the carriage, but they all moved on to congregate in another compartment further along the corridor.

Mr Ky waved goodbye and hurried off; he'd done his bit, and I was somebody else's problem now. The train departed on time and moved along a narrow alley hemmed in by houses and shops. A senior army officer was in the next door compartment. I noticed that he had two beautiful ladies ensconced with him as travelling companions. I bought a can of iced tea and a couple of sticky honey buns from the trolley girl and, later, a styrofoam-pack of chicken and rice for lunch.

All along the corridor mobile phones maintained a noisy chorus. I was sure the overly-loud accompanying conversations were no more exciting than the universal mobile phone exchange, 'Hi. I'm on the train at the moment. It's a bit windy outside.'

It was windy and cloudy outside. Over towards the west I could see a mountain range covered in thick forest. We came to a large town at three-twenty, but I failed to discover its name. The ocean and a long white beach came into view on the right soon afterwards. The sight created great excitement from within the carriage. A can of beer cost twelve thousand dong. I also bought popcorn and peanuts. It became dark at around five-thirty. The French people, jammed into a compartment at the end of the carriage were having a loud party. There must have been about twelve or fifteen of them. As I passed their door on the way to the toilet, I received several drunken invitations to join the festivities. I declined and went to bed in my narrow bunk. The rain and wind increased in strength, the force of it buffeting the train. Sometime during the night, three inebriated revellers came into the compartment and climbed into the vacant bunks.

Noises outside in the corridor woke me. Loud talk, laughter and giggles. It was dark; it felt as though I'd only just gone to sleep. I thought I heard someone mention the name Hue. Everybody out. I'd arranged to have a break in Hue for a few days before continuing on to Hanoi. As if in a trance I followed the others off the train. It was about five o'clock, black, windy and very wet. The train was not parked alongside the platform, so we all had to climb down onto the tracks and walk between our train and the one occupying the inside line before finding a spot to clamber up onto the platform. We were saturated, soaked to the skin, sopping wet.

The station waiting room was jam-packed with people, all shedding wet coats and shaking off water. I had no idea of what was supposed to be done. Outside the building the wind was so savage it was sweeping leaves, tree branches and sheets of roofing iron along the street. As I watched, the station's large windows swayed back and forth with the pressure of the wind and rain belting against them. I feared they would cave in at any minute. Across the road from the station, a building was steadily and surely being stripped of its roof. Against my feet, two elongated bundles began to stir and take on a life of their own. I was startled to see the heads of a boy and girl emerge. I'd noticed the bags there earlier when I took up a position in a corner close to a window, but thought them to be no more than someone's luggage. I could never have imagined they were sleeping bags with bodies inside.

After a spell of several hours, optimistically waiting for someone to show up and rescue me and cart me off to the Camella Hotel – the hotel Mr Ky had booked for me – I asked someone if he knew how far away it was. Perhaps it was just around the corner; perhaps I could brave the weather and make a run for it. I had to do something other than merely stand there, tired, wet and cold, and with no idea of what to do next. I showed the man my hotel voucher. After an intense scrutiny, he looked up at me and said, 'This is not Hue, this only Da Nang.' I was speechless. Astounded. My mouth hung open.

Nothing was happening. The occasional public address announcement – the ones in English – merely apologised for the delay. There were no taxis or other vehicles anywhere in sight. I overheard someone say the police had stopped all road traffic. I tried to see what the French group were up to, but they seemed to have disappeared.

'Can I get back on the train?'

'Where are you going?'

'Hue.'

'Where is your ticket?'

'I think I left it back on the train.'

And that was where that ever-so-slight offer of assistance came to an end. I spied another person in a railway uniform and approached him. 'Get on the train there, the one alongside the platform. It's going to Hue.' I realised full well that the train we'd arrived on was still sitting on the other side of that one, but I got on the one he indicated, anyway.

'Wait here.'

I was standing in the carriage vestibule, water cascading from every part of me. I was being jostled and trod on by people getting on and off, copping a fresh drenching every time the door opened. Then someone else came up to me.

'Where are you going?'

'Hue.'

'That train there.'

And he pointed to the next one over, the one sitting alongside, the one I had arrived on all that time ago. I climbed down and sloshed through the pools of water, only to find the carriage doors were locked. Back to where I started, to go through the entire procedure again. A while later, amongst the multitude, I recognised the conductress who had travelled with us from Saigon. Clamber back down into the fury of the typhoon and follow her along the narrow path between the two trains. She reached up and unlocked the door. I climbed into the train and found my cabin. Saturated, I shed as much wet clothing as possible and crawled into bed. The wind and rain never ceased. The train stayed there all day. The kind conductress asked if I would like something to eat. 'No money,' she said, taking pity on me and indicating that I needn't pay for it. But I was too sick to take up the offer. The words sore throat were taking on a whole new meaning. No one had any idea of what was going on.

Then, at six o'clock, a whistle blew and we began to move. Someone called out 'Halleluiah!' in a Vietnamese accent. We had been stranded for about thirteen hours. And, on top of that, I was beginning to feel decidedly unwell. However, our joy was short-lived as we came to a scratchy halt not long afterwards. I tried to sleep, but by then was so ill that all I could do was cough and shiver.

It was nearing midnight by the time the train made its belated arrival into Hue. The darkness, apart from a solitary glow coming from the station, was complete. Once again we had not stopped at the platform but were forced to climb down into the rain and trudge through puddles and potholes to get to the building. The couple of staff members still on duty showed no sympathy, nor were they interested in my plight; they just wanted us to be gone from their domain. On the steps outside in the darkness, a group of young backpackers, in as big a quandary as I was, were making phone calls to various establishments. A bossy railway woman locked the doors behind us and, with a decisive 'thunk', the lights went off. They obviously had their own power supply in there somewhere. And, they were not about to share it with anyone else.

'The whole town is cut off, no taxis can get through,' one of the young travellers announced. 'We're going to see if we can go around and get back onto the platform and find somewhere to sleep.' I borrowed a mobile phone from one of them and rang the agent in Saigon. Surprisingly, I found Mr Ky still in the office, even though it was then well beyond midnight. 'What am I supposed to do now? I'm stuck outside the railway station, it's raining, there are no taxis and the whole place is as black as the inside of a cow,' I wailed. I'm not too sure what I expected him to do or what assistance he could give me from so far away, but thought he might have some answer.

'Make your own arrangements,' he told me. 'And see how things are in the morning.'

'Make your own arrangements? Is that it?' I closed the phone and handed it back. The backpackers disappeared into the murk. I never saw them again. Which reminds me, I never saw the French tour group again, nor the army officer and his gorgeous, two-girl harem, either.

As I was preparing to wrap some clothes around me and settle down for the night, my back against the locked doors, and trusting that some kind soul would arrange for the removal of my corpse in the morning, a saviour emerged. A railway man appeared from out of the gloom and asked if I needed help. 'There is a mini-hotel nearby,' he said.

A mini-hotel? I was not familiar with the term, but I dutifully followed him for a hundred metres or more through the darkness and the slush along a potholed pavement. A room cost nine dollars. I thought it was the kind of place where the beds never had a chance to get cold. Like the rest of the town, there was no electricity and no water. I followed mama-san up a painfully steep set of stairs, trying to keep count of the number of floors we passed. As I followed the candle-light, I thought of Wee Willie Winkie in his nightgown. The room I was led to was on the top floor, in utter darkness and smelling a bit dank and musty. I crashed onto the bed.

From the window next morning, feeling no better, I saw a taxi standing in front of the railway station. The rain had stopped, but the wind prevailed and the sky was still overcast and threatening. When I approached the young driver he agreed to help, although, in my cynicism, I felt he thought he was onto a good thing and in line to make a killing. I had a booking for the Camella Hotel, I told him.

'No good, is flooded,' he said. 'But I will take you to the New Star Hotel. We should be able to get there. Leave luggage here, and if you like hotel, we will come back for it.' It sounded okay by me. In my dilapidated condition, all I wanted was to find somewhere clean and dry to rest my head. If I was about to be ripped off, then so be it. The streets were awash, the river, the beautiful Perfume River as described in my guide book, was roaring through the town, carrying with it tree branches and other flotsam thrown up by the typhoon.

Just to show that he was telling the truth, my driver stopped at a street corner and pointed out a building half way down the flooded block. The thick muddy water lapping at its entrance doors was about two metres deep. There was no way a vehicle could have reached it. 'That is Camella Hotel,' he said. Right, I believe you.

With my new-found friend's help I obtained a room at the New Star and we headed back to the mini-hotel to retrieve my luggage. The place looked no better in daylight. Rain came and went throughout the remainder of the day. Gangs of workers were out in force, clearing those streets that were free of water. The electricity came on again later in the afternoon. The air conditioning and the television in my room whirred into life. From a television news bulletin I learnt that what I had just been through had a name; it was called Typhoon Ketsana. It had made landfall about fifty kilometres south of Da Nang, and its first two victims were killed by falling trees and downed electricity lines. Maximum wind speed was reported at one hundred and sixty-seven kilometres per hour, with gusts stronger than two hundred kilometres per hour as it crossed the South China Sea and approached land. Knowing that what I'd experienced actually had a name did nothing to ease my discomfort. More news reports: one hundred and seventy-thousand people had been evacuated as floodwater rose in the country's six central provinces. Heavy rains and strong winds lashed a four hundred-kilometre-long coastline, causing massive flood surges in Hue. The typhoon killed twenty-three people during the first hours after making landfall. At least one hundred and sixty-three died as it roared across the country, seventeen people were missing, and six hundred and sixteen were injured. Airports, schools, communications and powerlines were shut down. Strong winds also destroyed parts of the north-south high-voltage power line, the backbone of Vietnam's electricity grid.

And, the final clincher: the railway line to Hanoi was out of action.

A hot shower and back into bed.

From within my damp luggage, I located the itinerary Mr Ky had prepared for me in Saigon.

Arrive in Hue at 9:10am. Welcome by the tour guide and driver, transfer to the centre, breakfast at the local restaurant. Hotel check in for the rest. In the afternoon, visit Dong Ba market, the Imperial Citadel from where the Nguyen Dynasty ruled between 1802 and 1945, and the ruins of the Purple Forbidden City. Enjoy the night boat trip on the beautiful Perfume River enlivened by a performance of Hue folk songs. Overnight in Camella Hotel in Hue. Breakfast at the hotel.

Take the morning boat trip to visit the royal tomb of Emperor Tu Duc, Thien Mu pagoda and mausoleum of Emperor Minh Mang, in a setting of gardens and lakes. Lunch at local restaurant. Free your time. Dinner on guest's account. Overnight in Camella Hotel in Hue.

I crumpled the piece of paper in my hand and off-loaded it in the general direction of the waste basket. I rolled over and tried to sleep.

Chapter Four:
Riding the Lhasa Limited

Of course there is no such train by that name – I just made it up.

However, there is a train that goes by the unromantic name of T-27 which takes two nights and two days to get passengers, including us, from Beijing to Lhasa in Tibet.

On the night we leave, Beijing West railway station is overflowing with people and their mountains of luggage; the city's entire population seems to be on the move. At first sight, the train is a disappointment – not the sparkling new high-speed, high-altitude model I thought we would be travelling in. The fancy Tangula was the train I was expecting. According to the Internet, it is a luxury train making weekly journeys from Beijing to Lhasa and back. However, I later learn, long after I've returned home, that the Tangula still has no official launch date, and everything has been put on hold due to economic hardships. Well, it's a bit late to do anything about it now other than grin and make the most of it.

We depart on time at 8pm to a chorus of mobile phone ring-tones and much hawking and throat clearing from our fellow passengers. Another disappointment: six to a cabin sees us stacked like cadavers on shelves in a morgue. Assorted pieces of luggage are stashed in every available nook: beneath the two lower bunks; on the floor and in the overhead space extending out above the corridor. This is soft-sleeper class and while it's nothing flash, it is the most comfortable way to do the Beijing-Lhasa journey, at least until the new, long-awaited Tangula Luxury Train begins operating. However, things eventually settle down and we manage to get to sleep on the so-called soft class bunks, narrow and rock-hard. At least we have been allocated the bottom ones, eliminating the need to clamber up the narrow, fold-away steps on either side of the entrance and stumbling over others in the dark.

I awake in the morning to a barren landscape beyond the window, brown and hilly with not a tree to be seen. I take note of the stations we pass through: Yi Wan Quan at 8.45, but find no mention of such a place on my map. Our fellow cabin mates, descending at various intervals from somewhere above, are friendly and helpful. One young and attractive girl gives us several sachets of coffee along with some mandarins, dried dates and Snickers bars. Her name is Wang Cui, but following what seems to be a Chinese trend, introduces herself by the English name of Tracey. An endless supply of hot water from a samovar at the end of the carriage ensures we can make coffee or tea from the teabags we have brought with us.

Still coming to terms with the train not being the one I thought it would be, I also have to accept that there are no showers, nor are there two-berth compartments. I also had some sort of expectation there might be an observation lounge car in which to relax and gaze out over the scenery: there isn't.

The train we are on is not for the faint-hearted, nor the less adventurous; it does not have Western-styled toilets. Personal hygiene is further hampered by the morning line-up of people, throat-clearing and nose-blowing, at the row of hand basins located near the toilets towards the rear of the carriage. My own thoughts of teeth cleaning and face washing are put on hold until later in the day. However, one touted advantage of travelling by train is the fact that one can slowly adapt to high altitude conditions instead of being suddenly exposed to them if arriving by aircraft.

A large black pipeline is running through the adjacent hills, as is a well maintained sealed road. At a service station standing alone in the wilderness there is a massive pile of coal and a line-up of trucks preparing to cart it away. Signs of a town, as brown as the surrounding landscape, come into view but are gone again soon afterwards. Farmers, rugged up against the cold, are tending flocks of sheep.

Yin Chuan Bu at 9.50, but still no connection with my map. I'm beginning to wonder if I'm even in the right country. We pass through many long tunnels and glide around high, sweeping embankments.

There is a prolonged stop at Dou Jia Guo (still no connection with my map) at 11.05 to allow another passenger train to pass. The hills are now much higher and topped with snow.

Hua Chang at 11.35 and then Zhu Jia Yao ten minutes later. I'm beginning to wonder if I'm looking at the correct map. At around midday we reach the top of these hills and the line flattens out onto a plateau.

At 1.05pm many people are making ready to get off at the next stop: Lan Zhou. I think I've finally located a spot on my uncooperative chart. This is a large city with plenty of good old-fashioned smog hanging in the air. The railway station contains many platforms. There is a ten-minute stop here which allows for a quick leg-stretch and a breath of fresh (polluted) air.

Thoughts of a late lunch in the train's dining car are almost thwarted by being told it is closed. However, the crew sitting and gossiping at several of the vacant tables, finally take pity on us and agree to come up with a couple of tasty meals, one of fish and another of curry with rice, as well as cold drinks.

Xining, the capital of Qinghai Province, is a major station. Our friend Tracey along with many others gets off here. We now have the compartment to ourselves. There is a long wait and we don't get going again until 4.25. From here on, this section of track is known as the Qinghai-Tibet Railway. On its journey from the Chinese capital, while still running over level ground, the train travels at a speed of one hundred and sixty kilometres per hour, but slows to one hundred and twenty when it reaches the Qinghai-Tibet section, reducing to one hundred kilometres per hour over sections laid on permafrost. This part of the line includes the Tanggula Pass which at five thousand and seventy-two metres above sea level is the world's highest railway pass. More than eighty percent of the line runs at an altitude of four thousand metres above sea level or higher. There are six hundred and seventy-five bridges, totalling one hundred and sixty kilometres in length; more than half the line is laid on permafrost.

We are now high in the Tibetan Plateau which, at more than five thousand metres above sea level, along with the Tanggula Pass makes this the highest railway in the world. The excitement of seeing my first yak soon subsides as more and more of the big shaggy beasts come into view. These great creatures are at home here. They have been domesticated and for thousands of years have been kept for their milk, fibre and meat, and as beasts of burden. Their dried droppings are an important source of fuel, often the only fuel available on the high treeless Tibetan Plateau. These animals cannot handle lower altitudes, and begin to suffer from heat exhaustion when the temperature exceeds fifteen degrees or so. Having larger lungs and heart than cattle found at lower altitudes, yaks are well adapted to high altitudes. Adaptations to the extreme cold include a thick layer of subcutaneous fat, and an almost complete lack of functional sweat glands. Butter made of Yak's milk is an ingredient of the butter tea that Tibetans consume in large quantities. It is also used in lamps and carved into sculptures for religious festivities.

Even at this height there are mountains higher still, steep

and snow-capped on either side. There is much new railway construction underway and many more long tunnels. About one hundred kilometres west of Xining, we run alongside Qinghai Lake for a long time. The largest lake in China, its salty water covers an area of more than five thousand square kilometres and is three hundred and sixty kilometres in circumference. It also holds an important place in history and culture as the traditional meeting place between Mongolian and Tibetan societies. On the very shores of Qinghai Lake in 1578, the Mongolian King Altan Khan gave the title of Dalai Lama to Sonam Gyatso, creating the first in the line. Because of this event Qinghai Lake is sacred for both Tibetans and Mongolians many of whose pilgrims complete the kora (a type of pilgrimage around a sacred site or temple) around the lake every year. There is also a small temple on an island on the western part of the lake. In traditional times no boats were used so the monks only had contact with the outside world when the lake froze over.

As the day draws to an end, I'm caught up in a welter of friendliness, generosity and curiosity, and an impromptu English-Chinese lesson in the corridor. The mountains, now higher still, linger in the background, slowly turning purple in the late afternoon sun. Hairy yaks are foraging in the sparse grass. Beyond the train's window everything looks cold and bleak. I sit for a while on a fold-down seat in the corridor, drinking from a tall can of Yan Jing beer and, through the window, watching the darkness close in. For a long time the fading light continues to glow above the mountains in the west.

Night finally arrives. An unusual document with a set of instructions on one side and a serious looking form on the other is handed to us by one of the train's staff: Beijing Railway Administration's Plateau Travel Instructions addressed to fellow passengers. It contains some alarming information regarding who should and should not be travelling on the train to Lhasa. Included among the do's and don'ts is the following: *The passengers can travel to the plateau only after finishing their physical examination and approved by the doctors.* Now this all very well, but by now the journey is more than half over. Reading further, I find that *highly dangerous pregnant women are not suitable to travel to the plateau.* We dutifully complete the details as required, but then nobody bothers to collect them. I could have succumbed to any number of *diabetes out of control, the hysteria, or the heavy sickness cold* and no one would have cared. I'm sure the documents should have been handed out, completed and collected before we even boarded the train back in Beijing. Were we meant to undergo a medical examination? Anyone admitting to one or more of these improbable symptoms could then have been told to make other travel arrangements. There was no advice on the form as to what we should do if we suddenly found ourselves succumbing to one or other of these contraindications while on board a train speeding towards Tibet. I wonder how many highly dangerous pregnant women have managed to sneak aboard.

We pass through the city of Golmud during the night. The one thousand, one hundred and forty-two-kilometre Golmud to Lhasa section was the last and the most challenging to be completed on what is known as the Qinghai–Tibet Railway. It took until 1984 to complete construction of the eight hundred and fifteen-kilometre section between Xining and Golmud. The line includes the Tanggula Pass which, at five thousand and seventy-two metres above sea level, is the world's highest railway, and Tanggula railway station at five thousand and sixty-eight metres is the world's highest railway station. The line also boasts some interesting tunnels including the world's highest: the one thousand, three hundred and thirty-eight-metre-long Fenghuoshan tunnel.

In the morning we are high in the mountains: a desolate landscape with patches of ice on the ground and snow-capped peaks in the distance.

There are fewer people on board now and we enjoy the luxury of having the compartment to ourselves. A constant parade of trolleys, each with its own supply of either fruit, drinks, hot meals and magazines, trundles up and down the corridor, pushed by an array of cheery women from the dining car.

I can tell we are at a high altitude as all our food packs have swollen. The individual sealed packets of biscuits have swollen and forced their container to take on the shape of a small football. Each time we open one, there is a hiss as the air at a higher pressure inside escapes. And, as a further reminder of just how high up we are, there are oxygen outlets at intervals along the corridor outside the sleeping compartments: all signs that we are climbing onto to the Tibetan Plateau, an enormous highland three and a half thousand kilometres across and sitting at an average elevation of five thousand metres above sea level.

We drift along the edge of a large frozen lake. I see more herds of yaks. A solitary hut has two motorbikes parked out front; a curl of smoke drifts from the little dwelling's tin chimney. There is no sign of human life. Yaks graze on the short yellow/grey grass that covers the plain. Then there is a school with an outdoor playground, but with not a house or other building to be seen anywhere near it.

We speed through Tanggula station, the highest in the world. There is a brief stop at Na Qu at 11.20am. Beyond the station, I see two men sitting on top of a goods wagon on an adjacent train. They don't appear to be railway workers, but surely they're not thinking of hitching a ride: jumping the rattler!

Jumping the rattler China-style

According to my unhelpful map, there should be another three hundred or so kilometres to go until we reach Lhasa.

Alone in the middle of a deserted landscape, a man in a bulky uniform, whether army or railway is hard to tell, stands to rigid attention and salutes as the train passes. Cakes of dried yak dung, used as fuel for fires, are stacked like fences in front of houses. More and more white buildings, stark against the brown of the hills in the background, begin to appear.

Running beside us on the far right hand side is the snow-topped Kunlun Range. Forming the northern edge of the Tibetan Plateau, and three thousand kilometres in length, this is one of Asia's longest mountain chains. An earthquake zone, dozens of earthquake monitors have been installed along the railway since a magnitude eight point one-quake struck here in 2001. A southern spur of the Kunlun Mountains also forms the watershed between the catchment basins of China's two greatest rivers: the Yellow and the Yangtze. These mountains, labelled 'The origin of ten thousand mountains' are a prominent pilgrimage destination for Buddhists from around the world.

On the highway, China National Highway 109, which has been alongside us all the way from Golmud to Lhasa, I see pilgrims wearing leather aprons. They pause their incessant prostrations along the road to look up and wave at us with wooden paddles on their hands. I am intrigued, but it is not until after our arrival in Lhasa that I can learn about, and admire, their determination and their unconditional faith.

Raised track over the permafrost

As we glide over permanently frozen earth on elevated tracks, I see dark brown tents and, outside on the grass, men in fur hats sleeping beside their motorcycles.

The closer we get to Lhasa, the more Tibetan our surroundings become. There are prayer flags strung across narrow, fast-flowing streams; others are hanging colourfully from poles out in the open or from the stone walls surrounding houses.

Dang Xiong at 1.15pm, then a slow and dignified, almost regal, entry into Lhasa on time at 3.25.

We have just experienced one of the greatest technical wonders of the modern world: the Beijing-Tibet rail journey. The Qinghai-Tibet stretch holds claim to being the highest railway ever constructed. It traverses unbelievably harsh terrain, uutilising some of the most complex technology available to overcome difficult constructional challenges. These challenges presented a combination of factors never before encountered in the history of railways, either in China or anywhere else in the world.

It is necessary for foreigners visiting Tibet to be subjected to a few conditions and jump through a few hoops before being granted approval to enter the so-called Autonomous Zone. An entry permit must be obtained and, worryingly, tour groups must consist of at least five people – all the same nationality. How are we ever going to round up three other Australians and convince them they should join us on a visit to Tibet? A major problem until the agent in Chengdu who is organising the trip emails me to say all is in order. She also sends a copy of the Tibet entry permit and a list of five people, including the three others who will be accompanying us. The list contains our names, ages and passport numbers. Interesting. How did she get hold of three willing participants so quickly and so smoothly? I began to look forward to meeting these compatriots; I felt certain that one fellow – who went by the interesting name of Christiansen Arne Norgaard – would surely enjoy a beer or several.

However, it is only after arrival at Lhasa railway station that all is revealed. As we leave the train, we are subjected to investigation by an inordinate number of police persons, asking to see our entry permit and asking about the remaining members of our party. It begins to dawn on me that there might be some slight problem. After being ordered to 'follow me' a number of times, we traipse around behind a policeman who takes some delight in studying our passports and showing them to his colleagues who then call others over to have a look and take turns at thumbing through the pages.

Lhasa railway station

We are escorted to a small, fenced-in office located in a section of the large open space at the front of the station. People waiting to meet passengers from the train are kept behind a barricade about fifty metres farther away. Locals and those with the appropriate paperwork are allowed to move off through a separate laneway and head out into the community and freedom.

Meanwhile, we are still following an assortment of policemen and women around, wondering if we will die of old age before a decision is made on our eligibility or otherwise to enter Tibet.

'We have someone waiting for us,' I manage to explain. 'There is someone here to meet us.'

Yet another abrupt 'follow me', and we set off for the

barricades where, hoping against all hope that somebody there is prepared to take responsibility for our future, I see two people holding up a piece of cardboard with our names written on it.

After a deal of discussion and more scrutiny of documents, including our entry permit just one more time, and a copy of the list of the others in our group, we seem to be free to move on.

As we walk with our driver and guide, who introduces himself as Ngodup (abbreviated to a more easily pronounceable 'N'dup') towards a car park some distance away, we are let in on how we are now part of the conspiracy regarding the minimum number of people required to form a tour group wishing to visit Tibet.

'The other names listed for your so-called group simply don't exist,' he says. 'We just make the names up. There's only the two of you. I told the policeman that the other three will be flying in later tonight.'

'How come the authorities aren't awake to this?' I ask.

'Well, so far, we seem to have no trouble in getting away with it. We want people like you to come and visit us, and it all seems a bit silly having to try and find three others before you can come.'

Chapter Five: Three Chinese Cities

Chengdu

The train for Chengdu retraces the route previously taken to Tibet. Beyond Lan Zhou, at a town called Baoji, the line to Chengdu eventually branches off to the south. Known as the Baocheng railway, this section is mixed single and double track. In 1975 it became the first railway in China to be electrified.

Linking with Chengdu in Sichuan province, it is the main rail connection between China's northwest and southwest. It opened in 1961 as the first rail outlet from Sichuan. With a length of six hundred and sixty-eight kilometres, it passes through mostly mountainous terrain and boasts three hundred and four tunnels and more than one thousand bridges, collectively accounting for seventeen percent of the total track length.

We arrive in Chengdu at 8.30 in the morning; it is foggy and cold. Chengdu is a 'small' city of only fourteen million people in the southwest of China. I'm here for two reasons: to say hello to the people at the agency with whom I'd communicated when planning the visit to Lhasa and, of course, to see the giant pandas. A most helpful young lady meets us at the station and takes us to our pre-booked hotel.

We arrange a trip to the pandas for later in the day, but it is aborted after an hour or more of languishing in stalled traffic.

By the time we eventually get there, if ever, all good pandas should be well and truly asleep in bed. I'm also concerned that this trip and the one planned for tomorrow are to be undertaken by taxi for which I'm expected to pay. Not an encouraging experience, going nowhere while watching the metre relentlessly ticking over. Then, when we agree to give it away, after another half an hour, it's back to the hotel through the endless and mainly stationary sea of vehicles.

This so-called traffic intrigues me. It moves only in great blocks between traffic lights. Green means a mass of vehicles, four or five abreast, proceeding as far as the next set of lights, where it halts again before getting a green light to proceed for one more block. And the Chinese love boasting about the number of new cars on their roads and how everyone is now rich and has ready access to a car. All very well, and I'm sure it makes someone feel important, but there is nowhere to drive the things, anyway. Who would be game enough to take his brand-new Jag out for a spin in this jungle? According to a recent *West China Daily* report, there are more than forty thousand people per square kilometre living in Chengdu and more than two million cars on the city's roads; more than in any other Chinese city apart from Beijing and Chongqing.

But I'm not here to comment on traffic congestion; I'm here to see the pandas. The city's Panda Breeding and Research Centre is the only one of its kind in the world located within a metropolitan area. Regarded as China's national treasure, the giant panda is one of the rarest, and most loved of all the world's animals.

Yesterday's traffic chaos has not abated; merely catching the eye of a taxi driver willing to forsake his spot in the great mass of vehicles is a problem within itself. However, after much waving and jumping up and down, we finally make it. And what a wonderful place the Centre is. The main attractions are a lazy bunch; lying on their backs and reaching out for a piece of bamboo. I'm sure if they had servants, they'd have them doing all this hard work for them. Their laziness also extends to crapping where they lie.

Welcome to the Panda Breeding and Research Centre

It was only in 1869 that the western world came to know of the giant pandas, after a French missionary first discovered the species in Sichuan. Now, the somewhat clumsy giant panda is a symbol representing the World Wildlife Fund. They are also a messenger of friendly communication between Chengdu and international cities. Chengdu's world renowned breeding and research base for giant pandas attracts some hundred thousand visitors each year. The Sichuan Giant Panda Sanctuaries, covering seven natural reserves, were included on the World Heritage List in 2006.

Though it is classed as a carnivore, the panda's diet is ninety-nine percent bamboo. In the wild, they will occasionally eat other grasses, wild tubers, or even meat in the form of birds, rodents or carrion. In captivity, they may receive honey, eggs, fish, yams, shrub leaves, oranges, or bananas along with specially prepared food.

Farming, deforestation and other so-called development, has driven the panda out of the lowland areas where it once lived in the central China mountain ranges. It is now regarded as a conservation-reliant, endangered species. There are around one thousand, six hundred giant pandas in the wild with around one hundred and eighty more being reared in captivity. However, the International Union for Conservation of Nature (IUCN) claims there is not enough certainty yet to reclassify the species from Endangered to Vulnerable.

The giant pandas have the typical body shape of bears. It has black fur on its ears, eye patches, muzzle, legs, arms and shoulders; the rest of the animal's coat is white. Although scientists do not know why these unusual bears are black and white, speculation suggests that the bold colouring provides effective camouflage in their shade-dappled snowy and rocky habitat. Its thick, wooly coat keeps it warm in the cool forests it calls home. Large molar teeth and strong jaw muscles come in handy for crushing tough bamboo.

The giant panda typically lives around twenty years in the wild and up to thirty years in captivity. The oldest captive, a female named Ming, had a recorded age of thirty-four.

In the wild, the giant panda is a terrestrial animal and primarily spends its life roaming and feeding in the bamboo forests of the Qinling Mountains and in the hilly Sichuan Province. Giant pandas are generally solitary; each adult has a defined territory, and a female is not tolerant of other females in her range. Social encounters occur primarily during the brief breeding season when pandas in proximity to one another will gather. After mating, the male leaves the female alone to raise the cub.

Panda playtime

Despite its taxonomic classification as a carnivoran, the giant panda's diet is primarily herbivorous, consisting almost exclusively of bamboo. However, it still has the digestive system of a carnivore, and thus derives little energy and little protein from consumption of bamboo. The average giant panda eats up to fourteen kilograms of bamboo shoots a day. Given such a diet, it can defecate up to forty times a day. Because it consumes a diet low in nutrition, it is important for it to keep its digestive tract full. The limited energy input imposed on it has affected the panda's behaviour, limiting its social interactions and avoiding steeply sloping terrain.

Knowledge of the giant panda first came to the outside world on 11 March 1869 when a French missionary was presented with a skin by a hunter. The first Westerner known to have seen a living giant panda was the German zoologist Hugo Weigold, who purchased a cub in 1916. Sons of US

President Theodore Roosevelt, Kermit and Theodore Roosevelt Jr became the first Westerners to shoot a panda while on an expedition funded by the Field Museum of Natural History in 1928. This was their second expedition into China. They returned home with a collection of forty big mammals, two thousand small mammals, six thousand birds and reptiles and to the amazement of their sponsor, the giant panda. This was the first panda specimen seen in America and the first complete specimen ever collected by a Westerner. They also managed to obtain a second panda skin, shot by a local hunter.

In 1936, fashion designer, socialite and 'animal trafficker', Ruth Harkness brought the first live giant panda to the United States – not in a cage or on a leash, but cradled in her arms. The cub named Su Lin went to live at the Brookfield Zoo in Chicago. In 1938, five giant pandas were sent to London. War brought an end to such activities.

By 1984, however, pandas were no longer given as gifts. Instead, the Peoples Republic began to offer them to other nations only on ten-year loans, under terms including an annual fee of up to one million US dollars, along with the proviso that any cubs born during the loan period were China's property.

Not all conservationists agree that money spent on conserving pandas is well spent. BBC wildlife expert Chris Packham has argued that the breeding of pandas in captivity is pointless because there is not enough habitat left to sustain them. He argues that the money spent on pandas would be better spent elsewhere. He says he would eat the last panda if he could have all the money spent on their conservation put back for him to do more sensible things with.

He adds, 'The panda is possibly one of the grossest wastes of conservation money in the last half century. Giant pandas should be allowed to die out. This is a species that of its own accord has gone down an evolutionary cul-e-sac. Unfortunately, it's big and cute and it's a symbol of the World

Wildlife Fund. I reckon we should pull the plug and let them go with a degree of dignity.'

Fellow wildlife expert David Bellamy agrees with Mr Packham. 'You can't release them back into the wild if there is no "wild" left, and we shouldn't be rearing animals just to put them into cages.'

If twins are born, usually only one survives in their natural habitat. The mother will select the stronger of the cubs, and the weaker will die. This is *Sophie's Choice* in the extreme. The mother is thought to be unable to produce enough milk for two cubs, since she does not store fat. The father has no part in helping raise the cub.

Having seen what we came here to see, it is time to move on to our next destination: Guilin.

Chengdu East Railway Station is massive. Divided into two spaces, the station building and outdoor squares, cover a total area of sixty-eight hectares. The main building is divided into five main levels, including an elevated waiting hall level complete with mezzanine dining and shopping areas. Ground level accommodates arrivals and two levels of the Chengdu Metro lines. The station has fourteen platforms and twenty-six tracks, all of which are under cover. Everything is neat and clean and new.

However, the train for Guilin, due to depart at six minutes past four is a disappointment, a direct contrast to its surrounds. Old and smelly, it is the worst we've encountered on our China travels. We seem to be sliding down the scale of comfort. Then, adding to our apprehension, the conductor shows us into a compartment already filled with people, including a very old man, two toddlers and their mother. But I can handle such situations. I've noticed compartments on either side of this one and still others further along the corridor are vacant. The lazy conductor obviously feels he'll have less work to do if he can jam as many people as possible into the one space. My argument, presented in Mandarin, initially surprising him, eventually convinces him, as does the act of running my suitcase over the old bloke's foot at every opportunity. Not meant to hurt him, but to demonstrate how crowded the compartment was. I've put my point across and we have the cabin to ourselves, space and comfort galore. Underway and out in the countryside.

Awake in the morning at a spot called Jin Zhou. Scenery is of farms and orchards, pine forests and red soil.

Liu Zhou at 1.50 in the afternoon. This is the southernmost extent of the trip. The train heads north making for Guilin, still two hours away.

Guìlín

Guilin is a wonderful city. One of China's best known tourist spots, it is tidy and clean, is relatively free of air pollution, and has many attractions. Chinese domestic tourists also flock to the area. What makes it special is its proximity to a multitude of picturesque limestone mountains and formations. Guilin boasts the most beautiful karst landscapes in the world. It is not surprising to learn that the main things to see here are all related to the rural scenery.

The place became one of the most important military, transport and cultural centres of China during the Second World War. The city's population drastically expanded as refugees from all over China poured in; by 1944 its population had grown from seventy thousand pre-war to more than half a million.

With so many attractions at hand, it is hard to decide on which ones to visit first. A cruise down the Li River is probably as good as any to begin with. I can tell this sightseeing destination has hit the big time; it appears on a banknote. The Li River and soaring karst scenery around the smaller, downriver town of Yangshuo feature on the reverse side of twenty-yuan note, along with the Great Helmsman himself, Mao Zedong on the other side.

We join a tour and are driven to the 'wharrf' (as our guide pronounced it) where a double-deck boat is tied up alongside. Here, several young cormorant fishermen and women are putting their birds through their paces for a group of tourists. There is more money to be made in posing for photographs than there is in catching fish. The cormorants have been trained to return their catch to the fishermen; a thread tied around their necks (the birds' that is) prevents them from swallowing their prey. But it isn't a spectacle for animal lovers. The fishermen sometimes give the birds a clip under the ear for returning empty-beaked. Poor things, but this section of the Li River has been overfished and pickings have become slim.

Cormorants on show beside the Li River

The vessel's upper deck is open-air while the lower one is set up with tables and seating. Upstairs, the passengers gather for photographs of the view on the banknote. The idea is to hold the note out in your fingers and take a pic of it against the actual scene. Sounds good, but all I manage to produce is an image of a giant hill and an out-of-focus twenty-yuan note at the bottom.

Li River views

Along the river banks, I notice that some enterprising souls have made use of the sheer sides of these hills by building their houses hard against them, co-opting the hill as a wall.

Another attraction is the Reed Flute Cave, a limestone cave more than 180 million years old, and filled with stalactites, stalagmites and other rock formations. Making it even more impressive is the multi-coloured lighting artificially illuminating the interior. Around the walls, more than seventy inscriptions of poems and travel stories written in ink have been dated as far back as 792 AD in the Tang Dynasty. However, since that time, the cave sat empty and untouched for a thousand years. It was rediscovered in the 1940s when a group of refugees, fleeing Japanese troops came upon it. Some twenty years later, the cave was formally opened to the public and has become an extraordinarily popular tourist attraction with people coming from all over the world to experience it. The cave got its name from the type of reed which can be made into flutes growing outside.

Sunday morning footpath entertainment

Sunday morning and preparations for moving on to our next destination: Xi'an. During our time here, we've become regulars at the Lakeside Café; a combination of beer, Wi-Fi and pizza being the trap. Although chasing pizza in a country with such gastronomical delights of its own should be regarded as sacrilege. On the walk there for the final visit, we are entertained on the way by a band of smartly dressed senior citizens playing stirring music. I'm sorry to be leaving such a delightful place.

Xi'an

The next train carries us on the fifteen-hundred-kilometre, fourteen-hour trip from Guilin to Xi'an.

To the dining car in the afternoon seeking beer. The man in charge of beer sales is also the man in charge of the trolley runs. I wait until he comes back. He embarks on four trolley runs throughout the trip: books, magazines and tissues; fruit; hot meals in foam containers; and soft drinks, crisps and peanuts. Beer can be purchased in the dining car, but, of course, you have to wait until the trolley man returns before you can get any.

Ten o'clock at Wuhan the next morning, we cross the great river, Chang Jiang (Long River) in Chinese, Yangtze to the rest of us. The railway bridge, built in 1957, is one thousand, one hundred and fifty-six metres long, with approaches at either end adding an extra five hundred metres to its length. Chang Jiang is the longest river in Asia, the third-longest in the world and the longest in the world to flow entirely within one country.

Xi'an is a dry and dusty city; water trucks are dousing the streets, mechanical road sweepers are sweeping and scraping. Trucks are being loaded with rubbish. Between the fog and the smog and the dust, a cough known as the Beijing Bark is endemic to this part of the country.

Running short of cash, I need to visit a bank to exchange a fifty dollar note. Customers at each of the three tellers' cages are actually seated on chairs and appear to have settled in with piles of documents before them, and engaged in serious dissuasion with bank persons on the other side of the grille. Mortgage, loan refinancing. No negotiating in the privacy of the manager's office; this is earnest, long-winded stuff. It is going to take some time. I check the number on the ticket I took at the entrance; it reads 52. The indicator display above the tellers reads 17. This is going to take even more time. I could die of old age before I ever see any money. Suzie, the helpful girl from the hotel who has led me here, shows her worth once again and beckons me to follow her to a man in the corner holding a brief case. Fifty Australian dollars for three hundred and twenty-two yuan. OK? Done. I'm out and away, business taken care of.

This city is world famous for two things: the Terracotta Warriors and the Giant Wild Goose Pagoda. The pagoda was built in 648-649 during the Tang dynasty and originally had five stories. It came tumbling down fifty years later. The strong-willed Wu Zetian, ruling Empress at the time, had it rebuilt and for good measure, and just because she could, added an extra five storeys to it. The structure suffered damage during the Ming Dynasty (1368 to 1644) while undergoing so-called renovations, and three storeys were removed. In 2014 it was added to the World Heritage List.

The pagoda acquired its name from a legend. According to ancient Buddhist stories, there were two groups of devotees, one of which enjoyed eating meat. One day, they ran out of meat and could find none to buy. Upon seeing a group of big wild geese flying overhead, a monk thought: Today we have no meat. I hope the merciful Bodhisattva will give us some. A Bodhisattva is a person who delays enlightenment in order to help all living beings achieve liberation (Nirvana). At that very moment, the leading wild goose broke its wings and fell to the ground. The monks were startled and believed Bodhisattva had shown his spirit by ordering them to be more pious. They established a pagoda on the spot where the wild goose had fallen and never ate meat again.

There is not much to become enthused over on the outside; seen one Giant Wild Goose Pagoda you've seen 'em all. But sections around the structure's base contain glorious artefacts and displays that more than make up for the mundane outside look.

It is probably rather mean of me to suggest Xi'an has only two things worthy of note; I should also mention it is home to the world's best dumplings. With a history of more than fifty years, these little gems have become famous. They are made in the shape of ingots, they are soft and they are delicious. Even the big knobs up in Beijing make regular forays – or send their minions – to grab some.

The foyer of Xi'an's famous dumpling restaurant

Of course, no matter how much attention is drawn to pagodas and dumplings, there is no escaping the fact that this is the home of the famed Terracotta Warriors. The brain children of the first Qin Emperor, seven hundred thousand men were 'persuaded' to go to Mount Li, thirty-four kilometres northeast of the city of Xi'an to work on a secret project The year was 246 BC. Two thousand, two hundred and twenty years later on 29 March 1974, a couple of farmers were digging a well on some waste land when one of them unearthed a life-sized terracotta soldier. The farmer had come upon the emperor's tomb and the mighty army he'd created to accompany him in the afterlife. For centuries, bits and pieces of terracotta had been found in the area, but none of it meant anything. Archaeologists had even discovered graves dug in the eighteenth and nineteenth centuries with terracotta discarded as useless and used along with soil as backfill.

Obviously, someone had to tell someone of what they'd found. The discovery was reported to the local protection department of cultural relics. They collected arrows and crossbows and broken warrior pieces to be restored at the local cultural centre. The restoration work caught the attention of a journalist who was in the area visiting relatives. His story attracted the attention of the government who, on 15 July 1974 established an excavation team to unearth the terracotta army. As we've been known to say on occasions: the rest is history. The first pit excavated to reveal its treasures was given the catchy name of Pit One. In 1976, the State Council decided to establish an exhibition hall on the site. During its construction, Pit Two was found. Then, as work progressed, another pit, Pit Three was exposed. The pits contain eight thousand warriors, thirteen hundred chariots along with six hundred and seventy horses. In the exhibition hall are two elaborately restored bronze carriages with bronze horses pulling them. It is all so fabulous and mind-boggling. The emperor, thirteen years old at the time he began preparing for the hereafter, made certain he'd have plenty of company when he arrived there.

Bronze horses and chariot

Time to say farewell and head for Beijing. It is Chinese New Year and everyone who is somewhere has to quickly get to somewhere else. The whole country is on the move. At the railway station a crush of people is funnelling its way into an entrance about a metre and a half wide. Girls on either side are frantically waving hand-held metal detectors over as many people as they can. A pointless exercise as the tide continues to surge through the narrow space. I catch the eye of one of the harried girls. She smiles at me and shrugs her shoulders, acknowledging the hopelessness of the situation. I wonder how many undetected guns and bombs have been carried through.

Chapter Six:
The Royal Way to Rajasthan

As my taxi stops at a traffic light, a woman spots me seated in its rear seat. She and her young daughter are sitting on the footpath amongst a pile of rubbish in the shade of a tree. Eyes light up; an elbow is dug into the child's ribs. The young girl leaps to her feet and throws herself into a well-practiced dance and gymnastic routine: bending, twisting and somersaulting. Then comes the universal sign for 'give me money': hand extended and thumb rubbing across the finger tips. Luckily, I have a universal sign of my own, also involving fingers.

This is Delhi, India's pulsating capital, home to an estimated eighteen million people and a place where every traveller needs to carry a sense of humour to survive. Often viewed by visitors as little more than a hellish introduction to heavenly India, there is much to admire about this town and its residents. Although lacking the beauty of Goa, Delhi has its own charms, even if they are dusty and decrepit. I think if India is going to get under my skin, it would be the taxi drivers and touts and shoe-shine boys who caused it. They hover in an endless swarm. 'You sir, where you from? Australia! Very nice place. Number one cricketers. Where you going today, Sir? I help you. I insist, my friend, please. Hello.' A one-sided conversation, one that was to be repeated in agonising monotony many times during my stay.

Wonderful things are to be found in the pages of Indian newspapers, of which there are virtually endless issues. One that takes my fancy concerns the administration of rough, frontier justice in Bihar. The locals, running out of patience with the criminal element, have started delivering their own instant justice by lynching suspected crooks. At least twenty-five people have been strung up in the past three weeks in the high crime-rate state. A senior police officer admitted they were aware of the rising incidents of lynching, both in urban and rural areas. 'In some cases the criminals were lynched even as the police looked on and family members and relatives protested. In some cases the victims clearly appeared to be innocent.' he told reporters.

Bihar businessman, one Mr Jagender Prasad said two men were killed by an angry mob in Patna last week reportedly trying to snatch a mobile telephone and other valuables from a doctor and some money from another man.

'Another suspected criminal was lynched in a village in Araria district. He was caught trying to break into a house. His accomplice, who survived, is in a critical condition.'

Another newspaper story bemoaned the behaviour of passengers on board a North West Airlines flight to Mumbai. 'What were they doing prancing up and down the aisle when the plane was about to take off and the instructions to fasten seat belts had been given?' the paper asked. Good question. 'And when you are told not to use mobile phones as is usual on all flights, why were they fiddling with them and passing them around?' it continued. 'Let's face it, we are an undisciplined nation and this is manifest in all walks of life, on our roads, in public buildings, in parks, everywhere. Go anywhere in the world, to the smallest country in the Far East. They may be underdeveloped, but they are spotlessly clean. You don't have to be a high-tech wizard to realise that litter has no place on roads, or that the ancient monuments we are so lucky to have are to be cherished and preserved.'

Maintaining its rage, the article continues in the same vein.

'The foreigner is a guest, but how do we treat them? From the moment they land at the bedlam we call airports with endless queues at customs and immigration, to the pushing and shoving that is needed to obtain a trolley, the very first experience in our country is a big turn-off. Then there is the dishonest cabbie who takes his guest all over town on a tampered meter. When halting at traffic lights, they are harangued by beggars, maimed and disfigured, little infants, bare-bodied and mewling in an emaciated woman's arms.'

Wow, amazing stuff. And it was not written by some disgruntled visitor, but as an editorial by a senior journalist. A couple of quotes I picked up have also stayed in my mind: 'The British might have invented bureaucracy, but the Indians perfected it.' 'Reality is a delusion caused by alcoholic deficiency.'

Beyond Old Delhi's bustling streets is the imposing Red Fort. This structure, held in the highest regard by Indians as a sign of strength, stretches for several kilometres and contains a surprising pocket of serenity in a jam-packed city. I see locals sprawling across the hectares of manicured lawns and meandering through the fort's old temples and museums. It seems the ideal place to spend a lazy afternoon and reflect on India's war-torn history and its colonial past. As fascinating and novel as all this is to me, I'm in India for a special purpose: to ride the fabled Palace on Wheels. Palace on Wheels – the very name says it all. This is India's most famous tourist train, giving a taste of royalty once reserved only for kings and queens.

On a Wednesday evening at the capital's Sadarjung railway station a traditional Indian welcome awaits and reminds me that I am in a country rich in culture. It is also indicative of the kind of treatment I will be enjoying for the coming week. We each receive a dab of red paint on our foreheads and are presented with a long-tailed turban.

Welcome aboard The Palace on Wheels

At precisely 6.30 pm the long yellow train eases out of the Indian capital and heads west. Along with a hundred or so other travellers, I am being fawned over and pampered to within a centimetre of my life. The train consists of fourteen superbly decorated coaches named after former royal states. The Bharatpur coach is inspired by that state's famous bird sanctuary. The relief work and white cedar inlay in the coach represents various species of birds. Its remarkable colour scheme, a blend of beige and aqua green, is every bit symbolic of the lush greenery of a bird sanctuary. The city of Jaisalmer also has a coach named after it. It is famous for its sandy landscape and rich people's homes, known as havelis. Accordingly, the colour scheme is the beige of the desert sand. Similarly, the other coaches have interiors highlighting the speciality of the place in Rajasthan they have been named after. The royal insignia of each of the princely states is also displayed in a prominent place in their respective coaches.

Of special attraction (and importance) is the bar and lounge car with its catchy colour scheme of burning red and gold, a reminder of the Mogul-influenced style of the Bikaner School of Art. There are two restaurants, The Maharaja and The Maharani. At the end of each sleeping coach is a private lounge: a pleasant spot with piped music, DVD player and the day's newspapers. Four twin-bedded chambers form part of each coach and contain facilities such as channel music, intercom, toilet, hot and cold running water and a shower. The train's boast is that it brings back the luxury of princely travel in the days of the Raj.

Underway, and I get to meet my fellow travellers. There is Louise, Mark and young Hugo, a New Zealand family living in Singapore, and Jonathan and Amy from Bermuda. The fourth compartment is empty. A card in my room offers the following information:

Leaving Delhi, the train cruises through some of the most exotic destinations in the state of Rajasthan: Jaipur, Jaisalmer, Jodhpur, Sawai Madhopur, Ranthambore, Chittaurgarh, Udaipur, Bharatpur and Agra. At each of these destinations, an air conditioned luxury coach will take you on a trip to explore the attractions of the city. These attractions comprise the gorgeous creations of nature as well as man himself. You will see the towering forts and elegant palaces that are the standing reminder of a bygone era. You will also enjoy spotting some majestic animals and colourful birds in the forests of the state. At various destinations, shopping forms a major highlight.

Night falls quickly. Beyond my window, in the gloom, I see

a group of men – their backs to us – squatting along a parallel length of railway track, not unlike crows on a fence. It takes a little while to realise what they were doing. Attending to their evening ablutions before going to bed, this mob is lined up in a row, enjoying a communal crap!

Day Two: Jaipur

We reach Jaipur, the pink city, very early the following morning. Breakfast is brought to us in the little lounge at the end of our carriage. Not too sure what we are able to order, we take it easy at first and settle for juice, toast, jam and coffee. As the days go on, we become more adventurous as we realise that no matter what we order, our private coach attendants seem to be able to provide it. By the end of the week, we're up for whatever we desire. I'm certain if one of us was to ask for curried camel's testicles garnished with braised peacock giblets, our man Mahdu would simply bow and say, 'As you wish, Sir.'

At the station a number of buses are waiting to take us away. We have been designated the Gold Group and given badges of that colour. On the way into the city, we stop for a quick look at the Albert Hall and its covering of pigeons before moving on to the Hawa Mahal, a pink edifice from where women could gaze unseen at the goings-on in the street below. As we step out of the bus, beggars and people trying to flog all manner of stuff surround us. Women holding up dirty, naked babies in one hand are gesturing to their mouth with the other, indicating they want something to eat. Scattered along the footpath, snake charmers are at work with their inquisitive cobras poking their heads out of wicker baskets.

The Hawa Mahal was built in 1799. From a distance it looks like a palace containing big, spacious rooms inside. Actually it is little more than a finely chiselled façade. Of its five floors, the top three are merely one-room deep, while the lower floors are connected to other rooms and a courtyard. It is an enormous, tapering structure with arches and spires and nine hundred and fifty-three latticed casements and small windows. It was designed for a single purpose: to allow the women of the royal harem, sitting in the cool, airy interior, to watch processions and gaze down on the people in the city going about their daily business through the streets of Jaipur. They could watch all the activity below while they themselves remained hidden.

Eleven kilometres from Jaipur is the Amber Palace. Elephants are waiting to take us on the slow, swaying ride to the top. The structure was initially a palace complex within the original fort of Amber. The fort, located high on a hill overlooking Maotha Lake, is constructed of red sandstone and white marble. On the ride to the top, the city of Jaipur, the lake and the original city walls all come into view. Once at the summit, a highlight is the hall of mirrors, dating back to when royalty lived here. At night, when one of the occupants was on the prowl and needed some light, he would take a single candle and, because of the myriad tiny, intricate mirrors, the entire room would become illuminated.

The jeep ride back down the hill is much quicker – and more comfortable – than was the trip going up. One postcard seller is so keen and determined that he clings to the rear of the vehicle, ignoring the danger while still going through his spiel, unfortunately for him, to a disinterested audience.

Lunch is waiting for us at the overly-opulent Ram Bagh Palace. I recall it was Rudyard Kipling who said, 'Providence created the Maharajas in order to offer a spectacle to the world.'

Then there is the mandatory visit to a carpet factory where we suffer and sit through a sales pitch that is never going to work and is wasted on a group of jaded train travellers. Carpet after carpet is flicked out and spread on the floor before us, the self-conscious assistants anticipating the 'oohs' and 'ahs' that faithfully come from their audience. Unable to stand it any longer, I slink outside. The edges of the streets are dust and dogs, camels and pigs, horses and goats. Great lumbering elephants complete the picture of this mobile zoo. Cows and other cattle of all descriptions lie wherever they want in the road, causing bicycles and motor vehicles to swerve and dodge them. A poor black and white milking cow, in sorry shape and with such sore hooves she can barely hobble, is being led at the end of a rope.

People are squatting and pissing against walls or in the gutters. An old man comes to the low wall beside a small park where I am standing watching several boys flying kites. Oblivious to my presence, he rolls up his trouser leg, reaches deep inside and drops out an old tool that has seen better days. Squatting on the ground and with as much nonchalance as if he was in his lounge room at home, he lets it go. He is so close to me that I need to move, certain the slowly encroaching stream is going to reach my feet.

I aim my camera at a man herding a couple of goats. He spots me and is not happy. In fact, he is so angry that he actually shakes his fist at me and waves the stick he is using to prod his goats. For one frightening moment, I fear he is going to come over and whack me across the head. Several boys approach, asking for money. A man kicks them out of the way and tells them to get lost. Then, as I think I've seen just about all there is to possibly see of the townspeople's sanitary habits, a little girl straddles the gutter across the street from where I'm standing and hikes up her skirt. Bereft of any underwear, she indulges herself in a hearty, old-fashioned, full-bodied wee.

Jaipur may be known as the Pink City, but when it was being built its colour scheme was a plain cream, and it remained so for more than a century. There are a variety of stories telling of the origin of the pink colour, but the one most agreed upon details the visit to the city by the Prince of Wales in 1876. Maharaja Ram Singh the Second, wanting his city looking clean and fresh to welcome his royal guest, experimented with different shades for different streets. Several colours were tried and rejected. Terra cotta pink was the final choice for the main shopping area. The colour stayed and gave Jaipur its name: the Pink City. There are now mandatory municipal regulations for homeowners to paint their dwellings in the approved shade of pink. However, there is a deal of confusion over the various pinks, ranging from a light ice-cream tint to a bright red. It feels as if the city is still not too sure of just what shade it is looking for.

Next stop, the Jantar Mantar is a collection of architectural astronomical instruments, built by Maharaja Jai Singh the Second at his then new capital of Jaipur between 1727 and 1733. It is modelled after the one he had built for him at the then Mogul capital of Delhi. He had constructed a total of five such laboratories at different locations, including the ones at Delhi and Jaipur. The Jaipur observatory is the largest. The name Jantar Mantar is derived from yantra, meaning instrument, and mantra, for formula or, in this context, calculation. The observatory consists of fourteen major geometric devices for measuring time, predicting eclipses, tracking stars in their orbits, and ascertaining the declinations of planets.

The Samrat Jantar, the largest instrument, at thirty metres high is the world's largest sundial. It can tell the time to an accuracy of about two seconds in Jaipur. Each instrument is built of local stone and marble, and carries an astronomical scale on the marble inner lining; bronze tablets, all extraordinarily accurate, are also in use. The observatory's main purpose today is to function as a tourist attraction.

Before being let loose, we had all received a briefing about beggars and begging. The good word from our organisers was to simply ignore them, and to *not* give them money. And, definitely on no account, even make eye contact. It sounded like the advice one would be given on how to avoid savage dogs. This is all very well but, obviously, no one has bothered to pass the information on to the beggars.

At the gates, as we leave this geometric jumble, the ugliest woman one could ever imagine is lashing out at a group of fellow scroungers and kicking them away from the door of our bus. The word 'crone' springs to mind. Of indeterminate age, this person is so ugly she could have represented India at the world titles. Her face looks as though it was created by computer graphics for a horror movie. The top of her head is bald, but a rim of straggly, filthy hair hangs down the back and sides and covers her ears. The shapeless garment she is wearing hangs open at the sides, exposing long, thin, dirt-encrusted breasts, hanging and swaying like a pair of leather straps. There is no fear of my making eye contact.

The state of Rajasthan is a land of diversities: forts, palaces, desert, sand dunes, game sanctuaries and wildlife. On the other hand, there are temples, mountains, green fields and colourful people. It is a region of battles, the abode of rulers, and the land of princes and fierce warriors who lived passionately and preferred to die rather than surrender and live. The origin of Rajasthan goes back to the Indus Valley civilisation (3,000-200 BC). By 400 BC, north India had come under the suzerainty of the Persian Empire which, in turn, was overthrown by Alexander the Great in the third century BC. By the eighth century AD most of the northwest desert was ruled by various clans in small kingdoms. Continuous inter-clan rivalry and the growing might of the Mogul Empire finally eroded their strength. Rajasthan is now the third largest state of India, and its most colourful.

Back to the railway station by six o'clock. At the carriage

entrance a boy pleads with me to let him polish my shoes. 'They're joggers, pal,' I say. 'They don't need polishing.'

The train has been serviced, this being its home port. The stewards offer us ice-cold towels with which to freshen up. In the room everything has been tidied and placed in order. A green, velvety bedspread adorns the beds. We shower, change clothes and make ready for dinner.

Day Three: Jaisalmer

During the night the train travels farther into the west. At nine the following morning we stop in the twelfth century desert city of Jaisalmer, home to artisans, camel traders and ladies wearing silk. Caravans of camels once arrived here from Persia and Afghanistan. The town's rich merchants built for themselves elaborate mansions, latticed and sculptured like giant wedding cakes. It all ended when the sea-trading routes opened and Mumbai became the centre of trade. Jaisalmer suddenly found itself a remote outpost, lost in the desert. By clinging to its proud past, however, it became a place where time stood still. The merchants' mansions, the havelis, have survived intact from the eighteenth and nineteenth centuries.

The vast fortress here in the Thar Desert is really an entire town, jammed with houses and towers, all built of the same honey-coloured sandstone. It is home to some four thousand of the city's seventy thousand inhabitants. Its narrow streets have been taken over by motor cycles and sacred cows. The pathways are slippery with mud from recent rain and fresh cow shit. Carved balconies reach out over the streets. A handwritten sign on a wall warns AIDS is not curable. Wear condoms. There are school children in large numbers, dressed uniformly in dark blue shirt and shorts and, in a monumental colour clash, long, bright red socks.

In the evening we head by bus forty kilometres out into the

desert for a camel ride. Beyond the vehicle's window the country is flat and sandy with patches of grass and small trees. There are pools of water, many camels, black goats and sheep, and shepherds caring for them all. I see square, stone buildings with thatched roofs. Further on we come across round, stone buildings with thatched, conical roofs similar to the Zulu houses one would see in South Africa. Goats and sheep aplenty graze around the huts. In the sand I see the remains of a disappearing fence; what remains of the stone posts, their wires long gone, stick up through the encroaching sand like a line of tombstones.

'The Pakistan frontier is only a hundred kilometres from here,' our guide announces as we select a camel and saddle up. Then, as if to forestall thoughts of anyone making a break for it, perhaps seeking a better lifestyle, adds, 'But the border is electrified and impassable.'

It begins to rain, gusts of wind torment me. I think this bloody camel has somehow damaged my bum crack. Something there is torn and beginning to hurt. And, adding to my misery, with every lurching movement of this ship of the desert the saddle pommel digs into my stomach with a powerful thump. Thick clouds roll across the horizon and block out any chance of a colourful sunset, the selling point of this exercise we are supposed to be enjoying. Please, just let it end. By the time we reach a camp set up to receive us with tea and coffee I'm in real discomfort. I've done myself some damage.

A strong wind bearing spits of rain adds to my plight. The wind, swooping in from the desert, is so strong that it is necessary for our hosts to hold a large piece of corrugated iron in front of the gas stoves on which water is boiling to stop them from being blown out.

Back at the railway station, a shoeshine boy is lying in wait again, offering to give me the works. In the dark he looks familiar. Surely it's not the same one who accosted me in Jaipur. Perhaps he has a twin brother.

Finally, the toilet flush mechanism in the bathroom has been fixed. 'It was the dust in the thing,' Mahdu explains. I think it was a bit more than just a speck of dust, but something I could probably have fixed by myself in half the time.

Day Four: Jodhpur

The shoeshine boy is there again, waiting for me at the carriage door. 'You promised …' he starts his spiel.

'How did you get here?' His ability to materialise at every turn intrigues me.

'Under train.'

'What!' I form an instant image of him each night slinking into some sort of hammock slung beneath the carriage.

'What did you say?'

'A nudder train.'

Right! Now I get it. So, a small army of shoeshine boys, postcard sellers and other camp followers ekes out a living of sorts by pursuing The Palace on Wheels around the country via a series of local trains on the off-chance of making a sale.

Yet another fort; I hope we're not to become 'forted out' before this trip is over. But the Meherangarh Fort at Jodhpur is extra special, looming spectacularly as it does over this fifteenth century city. The lofty fort looming one hundred and twenty-two metres above the city, is enclosed in imposing thick walls. High above the town, perched on a cliff, the fort is just one in a string of defences built in Rajasthan by the maharajas to protect themselves from attack. As we begin the five-kilometre drive up the winding road to the majestic fort, it becomes clear we are approaching something special. Even from the bottom of the hill, it appears vast, otherworldly, and impossible. The closer we get, the more I can appreciate just how magnificent it is. Rudyard Kipling described the Meherangarh as the work of giants, fairies and angels. Sometimes regarded as the eighth wonder of the world, its walls, up to thirty-six metres high and twenty-one metres wide, protect some of the most beautiful and historic palaces in Rajasthan. There are seven gates, including Jayapol meaning victory built by Maharaja Man Singh in 1806 to commemorate his victories over Jaipur and Bikaner armies. One gate, Dedh Kamgra Pol, still bears the scars of bombardment by cannonballs. The final gate, the Lohapol, or Iron Gate, is built at a right-angle to the road to prevent charging elephants from getting a good run at it. Should they have managed to get too close, the gate is also armed with huge spikes ready to impale them. Even elephants, apparently, are not invincible. Handprints, visible at the spiked gates, were made by all the widows who committed suicide when their husbands died in battle. The palm imprints still attract devotional attention and are covered in vermilion paste and paper-thin silver foil. The women had imprinted their hands in plaster, then, as custom dictated, threw themselves on the funeral pyres of their burning husbands.

The museum in the Meherangarh Fort is one of the states finest. It houses an intriguing collection of palanquins, howdahs, royal cradles, miniatures, musical instruments, costumes and furniture. The palanquin section displays a magnificent collection of the ancient royal litters. Palanquins were a popular means of travel and circumambulation for the ladies of the nobility up to the second quarter of the twentieth century. They were also used by male nobility and royals on special occasions.

The howdahs on display are a kind of two-compartment wooden seat, mostly covered with gold and silver-embossed sheets, which were fastened to the elephant's back. The front compartment, with more legroom and a raised protective metal sheet, was intended for kings and other royalty. The smaller one at the rear was occupied by a reliable bodyguard disguised as an attendant fly-swatter.

Whole rooms are filled with three-metre guns, swords and daggers. There are firearms, costumes, paintings and decorated period rooms. The ramparts of the fort, home to several beautifully preserved cannons, also offer a glorious view of the city's blue-painted houses far below and of the long, yellow trail of our train at the station. A movie is being made in the fort; cameras and lighting gear are set up amongst the cannons. Although everything seems ready to roll, there is no sign of any action, nor of any gorgeous Bollywood starlets.

The foundations of the fort were laid on 12 May 1459 by Rao Jodha, the fifteenth Rathore ruler. The hill on which it was to be built was known as Bhaurcheeria, the mountain of birds. Now comes another legend; I just love a good legend. To build the fort, Rao Jodha had to displace the hill's sole human occupant, a hermit called Cheeria Nathji, known as the lord of birds. Upset at being forced to move, the hermit placed a curse on Jodha: 'May your citadel ever suffer a scarcity of water.'

Rao Jodha managed to appease the old man by building a house and a temple within the fort near the cave in which the hermit used to meditate. Even though such action took some of the shine off the curse, even today the area is plagued by a drought every three to four years.

Jodha then implemented an extreme measure to ensure the new site would prove to be a good omen; he buried alive in the foundations a man called Rajiya Bhambi. Rajiya was promised that, in return for agreeing to be buried alive (as you do), his family would be looked after by the Rathores. To this day, his descendants still live in an estate bequeathed them by Jodha.

We move on to the Umaid Bhawan Palace for lunch. This

great golden structure stands high above the other buildings of the city. One of the world's largest private residences, it is home to the Maharaja of Jodhpur. If there is such a thing as too much luxury, then this must surely be it. As much a museum as a palace/hotel/restaurant/house, the place is stocked with an array of weapons and clocks. There is a stuffed leopard attached to one wall, and a huge banner presented by Queen Victoria hanging from another. From the extensive, immaculate grounds there are excellent views of the massive fort framed by the pillars of the palace. As I watch, a brace of F-16 fighter jets screams overhead; I would not have been surprised to learn they were part of the Maharaja's personal air force.

Beyond the railway tracks at the station, beggars, the crippled, the deformed, the halt and the lame are all gathered and lying in wait. The description 'wolf-boy' springs to mind at the sight of one poor creature on all (twisted) fours awkwardly loping through the throng, but moving faster than we can walk. I seem to be the only one who notices his passing. And, I do not make eye contact with him!

Back at the train by three o'clock and the shoeshine boy is once again lying in ambush. It's not that I'm unwilling to help him out; it's just that I'm wearing sandals this time and have no need for a shoeshine. Besides, he is really starting to get on my wick. From inside the compartment, I can hear him banging on my window and calling out. Next question, how come he knows which cabin I'm occupying?

The train leaves Jodhpur at half-past three, pausing at Sathin Road and then making a longer stop at Merta Road Junction. While propped up on my bed I had pulled back the cabin's curtains, all the better to take in the scenery along the way. At the station, a jumble of blank, inquisitive faces jostle for space at the window, cupping their hands against the glass, trying to see whatever there might be to see on the other side.

I slowly reach for my camera. They all spring back in alarm when the flash goes off as I take a surreptitious photo.

We travel through the night to Sawai Madhopur.

Day Five: Chittaurgarh

There is an early start this morning. We are now about one hundred and eighty kilometres from Jaipur. Everyone is roused to take part in a tiger hunt. We are given a breakfast snack-pack and directed towards a fleet of safari vehicles parked near the station; we set out for the Ranthambhor national park. During our drive through the park we come into contact with pigs and peacocks, we see blue-bill storks, deer and even crocodiles, but the elusive tigers remain well out of sight. Cold, tired and not really expecting too much action, the closest any of us comes to seeing one of the beasts is a set of fat paw marks in the sand beside the track. The Maharaja's hunting lodge presents a pretty picture, an exquisite piece of real estate in a clearing beside a small lake.

The park was established as the Sawai Madhopur Game Sanctuary in 1955 by the Indian Government and, in 1973, was declared as one of the country's Project Tiger reserves. Its deciduous forests were once part of the magnificent jungles of central India. Another fort, the majestic tenth century structure standing at a height of two hundred and forty metres, towers over the entire park area. The Ranthambore National Park is one of the largest and most famous national parks in northern India.

Back to the train for breakfast and tales of what might have been. As we step down from the safari trucks, we all hand our snack-packs and the remains of bread rolls and fruit to the crowd of young boys waiting for us at the station.

Around this time the sickness begins. It starts off gently with a few passengers complaining of the squirts. Louise in the compartment next door describes her room, containing ailing husband and son, as a Petrie dish. We are asked if we want to see a doctor. Recalling the dramas back in Queensland several years ago concerning an Indian doctor at the Bundaberg Hospital, the Australians among us agree they would rather wait until they return home. I make no mention of my damaged tail-end.

At Chittaurgarh later in the day there is yet another fort to be inspected. Thrice besieged, this one still wears the scars of battles lost and won. This one is called Vijay Stambha, known to us as the Victory Tower. It is Chittaurgarh's major attraction, constructed between 1442 and 1449 AD to commemorate King Rana Kumbha's victory over the combined armies of Malwa and Gujarat. Dedicated to Vishnu, this thirty-seven-metre-high, nine-storey tower is one of the most remarkable in India. Built partly of red sandstone and partly of white marble, it is enriched with numerous images of Hindu gods and goddesses. Each of the nine storeys is distinctly marked with openings and balconies. The entire tower is covered with architectural ornaments: the gods and goddesses, representations of the seasons, weapons and musical instruments. Its inscribed sculpture is a veritable text book of Hindu iconography.

The Indian people I meet along the way display a wonderful sense of humour; despite the horror of the terrorist bombings in Mumbai trains some time before I'd arrived, they are still able to joke. 'Why were the bombs only placed in first-class compartments?' one asks. 'Because the bombers couldn't find room in second-class,' another replies.

'How do you know the person you've invited home is a Mumbaikar?' asks another. 'The minute you open the door he makes a bee-line for a seat near the window.'

We pass through the town of Bundi, which also happens to be the name of one of the train's carriages. Piles of rusty steel railway sleepers are stacked up beside the line, buffaloes graze in the line-side paddocks. Tall rows of sugarcane stand in fields farther away in the distance. On the platform of the Bundi railway station a bulky, old-fashioned, sliding-arm scale sits alongside a line-up of buckets of sand to be used as fire extinguishers.

Day Six: Udaipur

It has obviously been raining; water is streaking back along the windows even though the sun is now shining. From my bed, I can see we are passing through areas of scrubby trees where cows are grazing; the usual rubbish and gunk lies beside the line. We reach Udaipur, the city of lakes, palaces, gardens, temples and – wait for it – forts. The sightseeing tour is due to depart at nine o'clock. Almost everyone on the train is now complaining of becoming sick; either a virus is sweeping through the carriages' air-conditioning systems, or the rather mundane and monotonous food in the restaurant cars is beginning to take its toll.

After lunch at the Lake Palace Hotel, the former residence of the Prince of Mewar, we enjoy a boat ride on Lake Pichola, passing two white-domed palaces surrounded by water. One of them, the Jag Mandir, is said to have been the model for the Taj Mahal.

I'm beginning to wonder if I'm not losing the plot. Enough of palaces and forts, at an art gallery we are taken to, obviously with the intention of looking at paintings and spending money, I find I am more intrigued by something more mundane. For me, of greater interest than a demonstration of how Indian art is created, is the fluctuation of the room's electricity supply. A large pedestal fan slows almost to a stop when the fluorescent tube hanging from the ceiling lights up. Then, the actions are reversed; when the tube begins to give up the ghost, the fan exerts a major effort in bringing itself back to full revs. Others in the group begin to notice as well. The vagaries of the power supply to the two appliances hold more fascination than a mournful lecture on how to apply paint.

Day Seven: Agra and the Taj Mahal

The final day begins with an excursion to the Ghana bird sanctuary, once the preserve of the Maharaja of Bharatpur, and now a World Heritage Site. Along a narrow, raised roadway we are pedalled in a convoy of squeaky trishaws by informative – and well-muscled – men who point out some of the three hundred species of birds living here. As well as the birds, lapwing, storks, kingfishers and the dreaded mynas (listed among the world's worst invasive species) well known to Australians, we also see deer grazing in the clearings. A sign near the entrance to the park proudly boasts of how the Maharaja set some sort of record by bravely murdering a vast number of birds, all in the one day.

Back on the train again and heading for Agra a couple of hours farther up the track. By now most passengers have had enough of forts: 'Seen one fort, you've seen 'em all.' Struck down with feelings of 'fortaphobia' in addition to their various other illnesses, they opt to go straight to the Mughal Sheraton Hotel where we are due to have lunch. However, I persevere and join those still standing for a tour of the city's famous Red Fort, the place where Shah Jahan, the builder of the Taj Mahal, was interned. Even if the Taj did not exist, Agra would still attract visitors to its Red Fort, one of the most magnificent of all Mogul palaces. Its outer public face is brooding and defensive, enclosed by fortified walls. Inside is a delicate marbled world of royal apartments, formal courtyards and audience halls. No matter where one stands, whether looking out from the Palace of Mirrors, where the women of the harem bathed by reflected lamplight, or the decorative pavilions above the river, the Taj is visible from every window. It was here in the Red Fort that Shah Jahan spent his final years gazing wistfully across the River Yamuna towards the exquisite monument he had created in memory of his favourite wife.

Through the grill in the window of his cell, I also gain a distant view of the famous structure. The Taj Mahal is the piece de resistance of the entire journey. Despite Delhi-belly rumblings, other creeping illnesses and relentless heat, all agree they will crawl there if necessary to see it. The initial sight is enough to stop me in my tracks. An ancient poet once described it as 'a teardrop on the face of eternity'.

Despite its beauty, the Taj Mahal can be regarded as a romantic impracticality. For two decades the resources of a vast empire were harnessed, not for the construction of palaces or forts, irrigation systems or roads, but for an elaborate tombstone. The result was the most magnificent construction in the great canon of Mogul architecture, a tomb with no purpose other than its own beauty and with no practical function other than reflection and memory. A building of pure sentiment, the Taj Mahal is perhaps the world's greatest monument to love.

To many of his own courtiers, Shah Jahan was considered a disgrace, an emperor in love with just one of his own wives. Never! This was precisely why there were vast imperial harems: to protect the empire from such a catastrophe. A man in love, so court wisdom went, was a man deranged. The intricate politics of dynastic succession did not allow for such mishaps. Jahan's beloved was named Mumtaz Mahal, the Chosen of the Palace. When she died in 1631 giving birth to their fourteenth child, Shah Jahan was heartbroken. For two years he withdrew, not only from public life, but from all the indulgence and luxury his palaces offered. Even before the regulation period of mourning was over, construction of the glorious monument had begun. Grief was being converted into architectural energy.

The Taj Mahal, its name a diminutive of Mumtaz Mahal, took more than twenty years to build with a workforce of twenty thousand men. An English traveller of the period wrote: *The work went on with excessive labour and cost, prosecuted with extraordinary diligence. Gold and silver esteemed common metals, and marble but as ordinary stone.*

Another visitor recorded his amazement at discovering that the scaffolding was built of brick, an indication of the limitless time and expense being lavished on the building.

When his son, Aurangzeb, seized the throne in 1658, Shah Jahan was interned in Agra Fort. There, he was consoled by the view of the Taj Mahal from the window of his room, and the stream of Tartar girls from the harem sent up to take his mind off his troubles. When he died in 1666 he was buried beneath the great dome, next to his beloved wife. The Taj is almost too gorgeous to be a tomb. Only when I pass inside do I recall its funereal purpose. In the gloom, shrouded in dappled light, the cenotaph of Mumtaz Mahal looks so small and narrow it could be a child's grave. Her real sarcophagus lies below, at a basement level, but it, too, seems disturbingly small and vulnerable beneath this great monument. Next to her lies the cenotaph of her husband Shah Jahan.

Near the tombs is a container into which visitors are expected to drop money. On my way out, a man in front of me deftly executes a slight dip, scoops up a handful of notes and slips them into his pocket.

Waiting for us back on board The Palace on Wheels are several cold Kingfisher beers, dinner and farewells.

Next morning, day eight, we are back in New Delhi, comparing our respective disorders and illnesses. I don't mention my very own torn-bottom distress; it's nowhere near as bad as what some fellow passengers are going through.

Chapter Seven: New Zealand

The flight from Brisbane across the Tasman Sea, as mundane as every other I'd ever experienced, was made slightly more enjoyable and memorable for two reasons. The first being the delectable meat pie, washed down with a couple of cold Steinlagers, I was served for lunch. I reasoned that only New Zealanders could come up with such a feature for a midday meal on an international flight. The second bonus was the views, firstly of the Southern Alps with their caps of snow dazzling sensationally in the mid-afternoon sun, then as we came lower, the green patchwork of the dead-flat farmlands spread out over the Canterbury Plains. I find no joy in travel stories that make much of views from aircraft windows. After all, it can be argued that everything on Earth looks the same from thirty thousand feet, but I felt my joy on this occasion was justified and deserved to be recorded. This was more than the mundane, much more than the usual sights that pass beneath the wings of an aeroplane.

A taxi driver sitting in his cab in front of Christchurch's International Airport complained when I asked him to take me to the Russley Hotel. 'It's not fair,' he whinged at me. He was a large, flabby Chinese man who, as I stood peering in at him through his window, looked as though he was on the verge of breaking into sobs. What had I said to upset him?

'I've been waiting here for hours for a fare,' he moaned.

'I've been sitting here all bloody afternoon, and then all I get is a six-dollar trip around the corner.'

Despite the cab driver's lament, I was thrilled to be in New Zealand on such a warm sunny September afternoon ready to begin my odyssey. When I inquired of the girl at the hotel's reception desk how far Christchurch railway station was from the hotel, and how best to get there in the morning, she informed me I would have to get a 'tehksi'.

The taxi ride to the station cost fifteen dollars. I was hoping the driver might be the same sorrowful man from the day before so that I could make his life a little brighter, but it was not to be. A fleet of buses was lined up in front of the railway station when I arrived there early the following morning.

Coach drivers were busily scooping up baggage and parcels from the footpath and sliding them into their vehicles' luggage bins. People, looking bewildered and uncertain as to what was happening to them, milled around. Inside the building I asked the lady behind the ticket counter the reason for all the activity out the front and the need for so many buses.

'They're here to take passengers on The Coastal Pacific to Picton,' she said. 'The train had an accident and hit something on a level crossing last night and it's still not fixed' (or 'fuxed' as she pronounced it). My adventure was about to begin aboard The Southerner, the train that connects Christchurch with Dunedin, three hundred and sixty-six kilometres to the south and thence Invercargill, a further two hundred and twenty-two kilometres beyond there. I had no need to worry about buses.

Train announcement, 'If you're heading for Greymouth this morning, you're on the wrong train.' It was reassuring to know that I was not on the wrong train, I was heading for Dunedin. The Southerner seemed exceedingly long when I first saw it standing alongside the platform, but I realised the reason why when it stopped a little way into its journey to unhook The TranzAlpine which was attached to it. It was two trains in one. As it made its way out of the station, the train I was on had dragged the other one in behind it. With the unhooking completed, train number 0901, The Southerner was suddenly reduced to a mere four carriages – three sitting cars and a luggage van. It left Christchurch on time on the dot of 8.15am.

The train was comfortable with deep lamb's wool-covered seats on either side of a small table. It was far from crowded; there was only a smattering of fellow passengers spread throughout my carriage. Taking up half of the middle car was a cafe selling a variety of food and drinks.

With the snow-capped Alps forming a permanent backdrop away to the west, we travelled along the edge of the Canterbury Plains. North of Ashburton the train crossed the Rakaia River over a bridge which, at one thousand, seven hundred and forty-four metres is the longest on the entire New Zealand rail network. The river, flowing in multiple interconnecting channels like a madly plaited pony tail, is known as one of the world's most dramatic braided rivers. It is also renowned for the excellence of its salmon fishing.

A card lying together with a menu on the table between the seats provided the following information:

> *A little further on you'll see the distinctive white stone buildings of Oamaru. Near Dunedin, "the Edinburgh of the south", you'll have the opportunity to see the yellow-eyed penguin, the world's rarest, and the royal albatross colony, the only mainland colony in the world. Further south we pass through Balclutha and Gore – the brown trout capital and home of country music. Invercargill is truly the end of the line; it's one of the southernmost cities in the world and has many historical buildings from the late*

19th and early 20th centuries. The journey covers five hundred and eighty-eight kilometres and takes nine hours. There are eight tunnels and three hundred and thirteen bridges, three of which are longer than six hundred metres.

We stopped for a brief spell at Timaru, a small town that will forever hold a special place in the hearts of Australians. For it was here that the mighty racehorse Phar Lap first saw the light of day. The legendary galloper was foaled at Mr A.F. Roberts' Seadown Stud on 4 October 1926. As we Australians seem to do so readily with so many famous people who come from New Zealand (apart from Russell Crowe), we simply claim Phar Lap as our own, failing to acknowledge his origins.

On its way out of the town, the train hugged the shoreline of Caroline Bay where I could see fishing boats, warehouses and large rail yards. A lighthouse stood importantly on a green headland, and deer rested in a line-side paddock. The train finally came to some hills, the first it had encountered since leaving Christchurch, and passed through a series of cuttings. The mountains over to the right had now turned dark and had shaken off their topping of snow. We crossed the wide blue Waitaki River. A marker on the adjacent highway informed all who needed to know that the South Pole was a mere five thousand and eleven kilometres away.

As it made its way out of Oamaru, a town of pretty white buildings and neat gardens, The Southerner was forced to tackle a steep climb and soon afterwards encountered its first tunnel. Train announcement, 'The cafe and bar will be closing in five minutes. We will be changing over with the northbound crew at Merton.'

Several minutes later, in a lonely piece of countryside the train stopped and waited until its counterpart pulled in alongside on the adjacent passing loop. The woman and two men who had made up our cabin crew did a nimble hop across the gap to the other train while their replacements leapt across to ours. We were soon underway again.

Newborn lambs gambolled (only newborn lambs know how to gambol properly) happily and starkly white in the green fields. Bright yellow gorse bushes lined the hills. We followed the coastline for a long time and at regular intervals were able to look down on its many beaches. The on board commentary informed us all that Blue Skin Bay, visible beyond the windows, was named after a heavily tattooed Maori chief.

'For the technically minded among you, the locomotives hauling our train today are a Dx and a Dc class,' the commentary continued. 'This tunnel we are now going through is the longest on the line between Christchurch and Invercargill.'

There was Purakanui Station, a tiny besser-block building, then Port Chalmers. Soon afterwards we pulled into Dunedin, on time and in drizzling rain. I hailed a taxi and asked to be taken to the Southern Cross Hotel, hoping that I was not about to throw another driver into instant trauma by wanting to just go around the corner again.

Dunedin's railway station is one of the most attractive I have ever seen. Apart from Kuala Lumpur's magnificent station in Malaysia, and not counting the great 'Grand Central' creations found in many of the world's major cities, Dunedin's is no doubt one of the grandest. It is a masterpiece, a fine example of how the renowned Oamaru stone – from the small town I'd recently passed through – can be put to use: in this instance as white facing to offset the hard stone basalt with which the building is constructed. The result is spectacular.

The building's most prominent feature is the tall square clock tower at its southwest corner, rising nearly thirty-eight metres above the pavement. The station's Flemish Renaissance style also compliments that of the Dunedin Law Courts situated across the street. The decorative features of both buildings give them an air of dignity and elegance, redolent of another era. The railway station was completed in November 1907, earning for its designer George Troup the prestigious British Architects Award, and eventually a knighthood.

Dunedin's railway station

I spent more time at the railway station the following morning, pottering around as I love to do at railway stations and looking at all the wonderful things I had missed the day before. In the tulip gardens in front of the building is a memorial to all New Zealanders who have been awarded the Victoria Cross. Dating from the Maori War of 1864 to the Second World War, twenty-two names are recorded on the monument. Amongst them, of course, is the legendary Captain Charles Upham who received the award twice.

Just inside the station foyer I discovered a plaque, known as the Passchendaele Plaque which, originally carried on

Locomotive Ab608, was later placed on permanent display at Dunedin. It now serves as a memorial to all the railway men who died for their country in the First World War. The main foyer floor is made of Royal Doulton porcelain tiles. Two stained glass windows above the balcony each depict an approaching steam train.

I booked a trip on the Taieri Gorge Railway for later in the day. There had been no intention of doing such a thing. Until then, I'd never even heard of the Taieri Gorge Railway, but after reading the brochures in the station ticket office, I was convinced of its worth. It was to be another wonderful surprise; I hadn't realised this at the time I made the booking, but I was about to take part in what must surely be one of the greatest train rides of its kind in the world.

The Taieri Gorge Limited left Dunedin at 2.30 pm. The train was a comfortable mix of new, specially crafted carriages and refurbished vintage cars, all of them finished in a pleasing yellow and brown livery. We followed the main trunk line south for twelve kilometres, past Carisbrook Stadium – the south's famous home of Rugby Union, known throughout the rugby fraternity as the House of Pain. Through the Caversham Tunnel, abnormally wider than necessary until I realised it had been originally built to accommodate two sets of tracks, but now only a single track remained and grass grew where the other one had once been. At Wingatui we branched away from the main line and headed northwest towards the Taieri Plain.

The train manager, introducing himself as Sandy, kept up a running commentary as we moved into deep green farmland and paddocks of sheep and racehorses. 'One of the horse studs just near here produced the 1989 Melbourne Cup winner Tawriffic,' he said. Sandy had ensconced himself in a seat beside the door leading out to the train's rear veranda, and spoke into a handheld microphone.

'Construction of the railway through here began in June 1879, but it was to be another ten years before the first section of line was open to traffic, and that was only twenty-seven kilometres from Wingatui to Hindon in the middle of the Taieri Gorge.'

Sandy continued his story, 'The Otago Central Railway originally ran through Middlemarch, Ranfurley, Omakau and Alexandra to Cromwell, two hundred and thirty-five kilometres from Wingatui Junction. In 1980 construction of the Clyde Dam meant the section between Clyde and Cromwell would have to be closed. Ten years later it was declared that the entire line would be closed. Around that time the mayor of Dunedin announced the city council would buy the line through the Taieri Gorge and as far as Middlemarch provided the community could raise one million dollars to finance the project. By July 1990 one point two million had been raised enabling the project to go ahead, making the Taieri Gorge Railway New Zealand's longest private railway.'

The Taieri Gorge Railway

At Parera, a remnant of New Zealand's rail heritage stood beside the line. There was once a passing loop here. The former station master's house, splendidly isolated and devoid of road access, telephone and electricity, is now a private, get-away-from-it-all holiday home. Although I could see no signs of people as we passed by, the recently mown lawn and a barbecue, tables and chairs set up in the back yard indicated that the place was not only inhabited, but a party was about to take place. I'm not sure how the guests were meant to arrive. From Parera on, the train followed the Taieri River for another twenty-six kilometres.

We passed through areas with delightful names such as Mount Allan, Little Mount Allan and Christmas Creek, named when a miner discovered gold there on Christmas Day 1863. In the midst of the Taieri River Gorge, the skill of the stone masons could be appreciated to full effect on the grand viaducts that carried the train far above the river. We paused for a while at a spot called Hindon, still in use as a crossing place for trains going in either direction. Sandy told us there used to be refreshment rooms there until they burned down in 1949. From there on, the train climbed ever higher above the river.

I looked forward to Sandy's promise of a stop for refreshments at the Reefs Hotel, only to be slightly disappointed – I felt sure all along that it was too good to be true – to find it was nothing more than a small wooden shed perched high on a rocky ledge above the gorge. Some wag had long ago painted the words 'Reefs Hotel' above the door. On a rock face in the stone cutting leading out of the Reefs there was a bronze plaque. It was a memorial to the pilot of a light aircraft who several years earlier had flown along the gorge in a light aircraft and, obviously with his mind on other things at a crucial stage of the flight, had misjudged his altitude.

A short while later, we stopped at Pukerangi, forty-five

kilometres from Wingatui and two hundred and fifty metres above sea level. This was the end of the run and the place where most of the passengers left the train to continue their journey across country to Queenstown on the buses that were lined up ready and waiting. We had moved out of the gorge and were sitting at a small wooden station on the top of an open, almost flat, treeless plain. Sandy told us that the word Pukerangi meant Hill of Heaven. 'Although, I can never quite work out what's supposed to be heavenly about it,' he added.

Trying not to sound too sycophantic, I said to him that the trip was better than the famous Kuranda Tourist Train in North Queensland. My feelings of guilt over being such a traitor to my home state vanished when he responded by asking if I'd like to ride in the cab of the loco on the return trip. Would I! I climbed up into the engine with driver Ross and his offsider Jarrod. Easing back down around the cliff faces, we followed the river, crossed the iron and stone viaducts again, all the while herding errant goats and sheep as they strayed into the train's path.

The following day I was ready to move on. I awoke to a gloriously sunny morning. Members of the Dunedin Jaguar Car Club were celebrating something or other with a display of their cherished cars in the Octagon: the eight-sided 'square' that forms the city centre. The club members had even baked several cakes and were offering pieces to the onlookers and passers-by. I'd intended to visit the Otago Settlers Museum before boarding my train but was dismayed to find it closed on weekends; surely, one would think, the very time when museums of any description did most of their business.

Returning disappointed to the Octagon, I sat at a sidewalk table in the warm sunshine, drinking coffee, eating Jaguar Car Club chocolate cake, and listening to the birdlike trills of the traffic lights as they changed colour at the nearby pedestrian crossings. Mark Twain seemed to have summed up the wonder of this place in the comment he made in 1895, describing Dunedin and its inhabitants in his book *Following the Equator* as, 'The people are Scotch; they stopped here on their way to heaven, thinking they had arrived.'

Back at the station another Southerner duly arrived to take me on the next leg of my trip to Invercargill. It retraced the path of yesterday's journey; past the great stadium, through the overly-wide tunnel yet again and Wingatui Junction where the line had branched away to Taieri Gorge. We continued south, running for a long time beside Lake Waihola and endless green fields dotted with sheep. Gorse and broom bushes added their golden glow to the hillsides. The carriages on this train were different from the ones I had travelled in on the way down to Dunedin. There were no tables situated between opposite-facing seats; this time we were all pointed in the same direction. Metal trays stuck in the pockets at the back of the seats in front had to be juggled into a slot in the arm rest of your seat if you wanted a place on which to write notes to someone, or spread out magazines and whatnots, or sandwiches and coffee.

We made a brief stop at Milton, then Galclutha where its wide river was spanned by a large steel bridge. Train announcement, 'The cafe counter will be closing when we reach Gore which will be in about fifteen minutes time.'

We pulled into Gore at 4.15pm. An oversized guitar stuck on a pedestal in the town's deserted main street proclaimed to all and sundry that this was the nation's country music capital. A big fish stuck on a stick nearby also served as a reminder that the area is the World Capital of Brown Trout Fishing.

The on board commentary relayed a tale of an illicit whiskey industry that was once conducted here, 'The early Scottish settlers brought with them their liking for a daily drop or two of Highland Dew. With the advent of prohibition in the 1900s, the demand for the by then well-established

Hokonui Moonshine grew. Stills sprang up in the hills around the town and the authorities staged many a raid trying to put an end to the illicit goings-on. Even though it was illegal, there still remains an aura of romance and mystique about it all.'

Also in Gore's main street were the familiar red and white stripes of a KFC restaurant, always a good sign that a town has made it! On the edge of town at a sports club, groups of men dressed in white and huddled together like worrisome doctors at each end of bowling rinks, were intensely engaged in a game of lawn bowls. As I watched them from the train window, there came to me the reminder that this day really was a Saturday afternoon. The scene could have been repeated in any country town or city in Australia. I imagined I could hear the skips calling instructions to their team mates at the opposite ends of the greens. At least the correct day of the week was now programmed firmly into my mind; my in-built calendar was operating once again. Ever since I'd arrived in New Zealand, every day had felt like a Saturday afternoon.

The small siding of Mataura boasts a fine old, wooden station building that has been out of use for many years. Along the sides of the highway and the railway line there were no advertising billboards; visual pollution was simply not part of this landscape. All that was to be seen was the unhindered and continuing greenness of the sheep farms. At Edendale, the home of New Zealand's cheese industry since 1881, the small wooden station building had long ago been boarded up and abandoned. Its paint had peeled and the name of the station was barely visible on the platform.

I stayed a couple of days in Invercargill, not too sure what I was doing there, but reasoning that if this was where the railway line ended, then this was where I should be. Invercargill regards itself as the City of Water and Light. The light referring to the long summer twilights and the Aurora

Australis (the Southern Lights). Apparently, local jokers included the water part in the name because of the notorious horizontal, driving rain in high wind at the corner of the town's two main streets: Dee and Tay.

I spent Sunday morning walking the gravel paths threading between neat flower beds in Queens Park. This glorious park was also home to a Tuatara, a lizard-like reptile endemic to New Zealand.

A Tuatara in Invercargill's Queen's Park

The day was bleak and cold, with a half-hearted sun making no impact on the temperature. After morning tea in the gardens' kiosk, I looked through the adjacent aviary and visited the Southland Museum and Art Gallery. An excellent meal in the Frog and Ferkin Restaurant later in the day was enhanced by its old-English pub charm. I was amused, if not a little dismayed by a sign on the wall which caught my attention. It read: *If we don't have you in and out within the hour at lunch time, we guarantee you will be late back to work.*

With nothing better to do, and looking for an escape from the cold, I went to the movies, something I would normally never do. However, the novelty here lay in the fact that this cinema bills itself as the world's southernmost picture theatre. I can't remember what the movie was, and I don't particularly want to know. But having seen it, I felt I had also seen all there was to see of Invercargill.

The Southerner was an express passenger train operating in New Zealand's South Island, running between Christchurch and Invercargill along the South Island Main Trunk. It operated from 1970 to 2002. One of New Zealand's premier passenger trains, its existence made Invercargill the southernmost passenger station in the world. According to Wikipedia, that honour now belongs to a station in Tierra del Fuego Province, Argentina.

The End

Also by Jim Nicholls

A Country Corps
(A history of the Salvation Army in the Lockyer Valley)

The Runaway Rattler
(A novel tracing the adventures of a lone traveller circumnavigating the world by trains) See review included

*Murder in the Rain
(The true local crime story of a 1933 murder)

Tales of Travel and Trains

An Aussie in Asia

The Magic of Myanmar
(A pictorial journey through a golden land)

Africa, the train the covenant
(A train journey from Naminia to Pretoria interspersed with Southern African history)

Ukraine
(Notes from a fractured land)

Taking the world by train

*Glenore Grove and the body in the billabong
(A re-write of Murder in the Rain)

About the Author

Jim Nicholls was born in Cootamundra NSW where, as a young boy his fascination with all things railway began.

After a 21-year-stint in the Royal Australian Air Force, he moved with his family to Laidley in Queensland where he took up a position in the Administration Department of the nearby Queensland Agricultural College.

Turning his hand to writing, he served as the long-time country correspondent for the major regional newspaper *The Queensland Times*. For many years he was also the chief reporter for the Laidley-based *Valley Weekender*.

He has travelled the world in search of adventure and train travel, producing stories from the Trans-Siberian Railway, USA, UK, South America, Africa, China, Tibet, India, Myanmar, Ukraine and South-East Asia. And, of course his home country of Australia.

He is the author of several popular books, and has had his many history and travel stories featured in a variety of publications.

In 2003 his literary efforts were recognised with the Laidley Shire Council's award of their Australia Day Cultural Medal.

Prior to retirement, and the corona virus shutdowns, he enjoyed visiting distant places and writing about them on his return.

www.ingramcontent.com/pod-product-compliance
Lightning Source LLC
LaVergne TN
LVHW011949070526
838202LV00054B/4854